William Stanley - A Yorkist Martyr?

by

Jean M. Gidman

Leeds
ROSALBA PRESS
2003

"Rosalba Press"
is the publishing group of
the Yorkshire Branch of the Richard III Society

18 St.Martin's Drive, Leeds, LS7 3LR

AUTHOR'S NOTE

WHEN I first came to Lancashire in 1974 the late Pauline Routh suggested that as they were on the doorstep I should "look into the Stanley's." I decided to concentrate my researches on Sir William Stanley, as less was known about him than his brother Thomas. Since then a great deal has been written about them and the various incidents that they were concerned with. However no attempt has been made to look at Sir William as the central subject. This I have endeavoured to rectify.

In writing the following I am grateful to Pauline and to the late Arthur Cockerill for their encouragement at the start, to Mary O'Regan for her help with the Inventory; the Librarians and staff at Ormskirk Public Library, Edge Hill University College and Liverpool University for their help; to my friends for their support, and my husband who has accompanied me on Sir William Stanley hunts through Cheshire and North Wales. My thanks also go to Mary Tetlow for her drawings. The opinions and errors are mine.

Edited and designed by Mary O'Regan

ISBN: 0 907604 06 4

CONTENTS

LIST OF ILLUSTRATIONS

Ancestors of Sir William Stanley

William = 1282 **Joan**, dau. of Sir Philip de **Bamville** of Storeton
(circa 1250-1324) |

John (circa 1285-circa 1330) = 1310 **Emma Molyneux**
|

Alice Massey = 1330 **William** (circa 1310-60)
|

John = 1385 **Isabel Lathom** (circa 1355-
(circa1340-Jan.1413/14) | Oct.1414)

John = **Isabel Harrington**
(circa 1386-1437) |

Thomas = **Joan**, dau. Robert **Goushill**
(circa 1405-59) |

WILLIAM born about 1436
married (1) about 12 November 1465
and (2) some time after 1470
died 16 February 1494/95, Tower of London

Descendants of Sir William Stanley

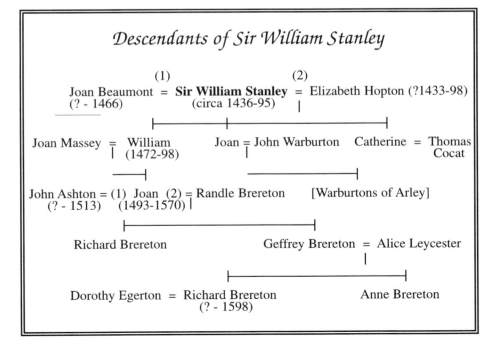

(1) (2)
Joan Beaumont = **Sir William Stanley** = Elizabeth Hopton (?1433-98)
(? - 1466) (circa 1436-95) |

Joan Massey = William Joan = John Warburton Catherine = Thomas
| (1472-98) | Cocat

John Ashton = (1) Joan (2) = Randle Brereton [Warburtons of Arley]
(? - 1513) (1493-1570) |

Richard Brereton Geffrey Brereton = Alice Leycester
|

Dorothy Egerton = Richard Brereton Anne Brereton
(? - 1598)

iv

Chapter One[1]

Ancestry and Early Life

WHEN William Stanley left with his men in September 1459 to fight for the Yorkist cause at Blore Heath he was following a family tradition which extended back to his great-grandfather Sir John Stanley (I) and even further.

The surname can be traced to Stanley, about five miles south-west of Leek in Staffordshire. The earliest mention of the house of Stanley which so far has been discovered is a reference of c.1200 when one *"Adam son of Lydulf de Aldelegha [Audley] grants to William de Standlegha son of Adam de Standlegha uncle of grantor all Standlegh with appurtenances etc which belonged to grantor, for twelve pence of annual rent etc."* From there they moved to Storeton on the Wirral, when **William** de Stanley married Joan, the eldest of three daughters and co-heiresses of Sir Philip de Bamville of Storeton, Chief Forester of Wirral in 1282.[2] It was William who was granted, by Edward II in 1316, three buck's heads for his arms or bearings.[3]

Sir **John** Stanley (born c.1340) was the great-grandson of that William and was a younger son. His elder brother William (IV) inherited the Storeton estates. John, therefore, sought to marry the heiress of Lathom, Isabel de Lathom, in 1385 when he was about forty-five years of age.[4]

It was during the political crisis of 1399 when Henry Duke of Lancaster laid claim to the estates of his father John of Gaunt that Sir John Stanley made the decision to oppose the anointed king and follow the Lancastrian banner.[5]

Under Henry IV Sir John was even more enriched. He received more estates in Cheshire as a reward for his support and in 1405 was granted the Lordship of Man in exchange for the loyal support he gave the king during the Percys' rebellion (his nephew William [V] had supported the Percys).[6] Initially this grant was for life only, but in 1406 in exchange for a payment of 1,300 marks it was made hereditary, and to it was added the Captaincy of Castle Rushen and the patronage of the bishopric of Sodor and Man. This was worth about £400 per annum to Sir John. Finally, also in 1406, he was made Knight of the Garter. In Lancashire he acquired the right of free warren on his Lathom, Knowsley, Roby, Childwall, and Anglezarke estates. He was also allowed to fortify his house in Liverpool, which he was building on the waterfront and which became known as Stanley's Tower. In 1408 Henry IV sent Sir John back to Ireland, this time as Lord Lieutenant, where he died six years later on or about 28 January 1414.[7] His body was brought back to Lancashire and buried in Burscough Priory.[8]

Sir John Stanley's and Isabel's son and heir was another Sir **John**, who was born c.1386. He took as his crest the eagle and child of the Lathoms and placed the Lathom arms - *Or, on a chief indented azure three plates* - on his shield in the first and fourth quarters, and the Stanley arms - *Argent, on a bend azure three stag's heads cabossed or* - in the second and third quarters, thus giving his mother's arms precedence and showing that he acknowledged that most of his estates had been inherited from her. Sir John was not the soldier that his father had been. He represented Lancashire as one of its two MPs in the first two Parliaments of the reign of Henry V. But when it came to war he stayed at home.

He served as Justice of Chester and Master Forester of the Forests of Macclesfield and Delamere and bought more land and the advowsons of many churches, thus extending his family's influence in Lancashire, Cheshire and North Wales. He did, however, serve in France at the siege and capture of Rouen in 1418. He married Isabel, daughter of Sir Nicholas Harrington of Farleton in the Lune Valley. He died in 1437 and was succeeded by his son **Thomas**.[9]

Thomas was born c.1406 and knighted c.1429. Henry V had died in 1422 leaving his heir, Henry VI, a child of under a year old. This led to faction and dispute as to who should govern in the king's name. After his father's death Sir Thomas was appointed Lord Lieutenant of Ireland for six years, and in the 1440s and 1450s he too represented Lancashire in the House of Commons. Henry VI trusted and favoured him and appointed him Chamberlain and Comptroller of the Royal Household in 1448, raising him to the rank of Baron Stanley in 1456. At the time of the First Battle of St. Albans in 1455 he mobilized a large army of Cheshire men but arrived too late to take part in the battle. Thus, being an astute politician, he was careful not to commit himself to either side, a trait that was adopted to advantage by his son Thomas.[10] In 1457 he was admitted to the Order of the Garter. He married Joan, daughter and heiress of both her father Sir Robert Goushill of Hoveringham, Nottinghamshire and of her mother Elizabeth, daughter of the Earl of Arundel; they had seven children.[11] He died in February 1459 and was buried at Burscough Priory.[12]

Lord Stanley's heir, his eldest son **Thomas**, who became the second Lord Stanley, was born in 1433, and three brothers and three sisters followed. His brothers were

- **William** (the subject of this work)
- **John**, who married Elizabeth daughter and heiress of Sir Thomas Weever of Weever, co. Chester, and from whom the Barons Stanley of Alderley are descended, and
- **James** who became Archdeacon of Carlisle.

His sisters were

- **Margaret**, who married Sir William Troutbeck of Cheshire, killed at Blore Heath in 1459[13]
- **Elizabeth**, who married Sir Richard Molyneux of Sefton[14] and

- **Catharine**, who married Sir John Savage and is buried in Macclesfield.[15]

On the death of Thomas Stanley, 1st Lord Stanley, in February 1459, many of his offices in both Lancashire and Cheshire were transferred to others, including the Justiceship of Chester which was given to John Talbot, 2nd Earl of Shrewsbury. Sir Richard Tunstall became Baron of the Lancaster Exchequer and Receiver of the Palatinate, and also Chamberlain of the Household.[16]

The struggle for power in the land had manifested itself in the First Battle of St. Albans on 22 May 1455, when Richard Duke of York had defeated the forces of Henry VI and had taken control of the government. An uneasy truce had resulted which ended in 1457 when Margaret of Anjou, the wife of Henry VI, seized back power. However, this was not going to be the end of the struggle. Despite an elaborate reconciliation at St Paul's church in London in 1458 both parties prepared for renewed hostilities.

Matters came to a head in 1459 when in September Richard Neville, Earl of Salisbury, left his stronghold of Middleham Castle in Wensleydale in Yorkshire to join forces with his brother-in-law, the Duke of York, at Ludlow. The Lancastrians (the supporters of the king) sent out a force of Cheshire men under Lord Audley to intercept them and the two armies met just south of the Cheshire-Staffordshire border at Blore Heath on 23 September 1459.

To this battle went young William Stanley. He was probably in his early twenties, having been born some time after 1435.[17] The family, having managed to avoid being directly involved in the First Battle of St Albans, was now presented four years later with a repeat of the situation. Thomas, newly become Lord Stanley, performed the first of a series of non-interventions which typified the rest of his life and echoed his father's behaviour of four years earlier. While setting out for the battle he arrived too late to take part. He had married the daughter of the Earl of Salisbury, Eleanor Neville, and was thus brother-in-law to the Earl of Warwick, but this had not made him any more anxious to commit himself to one side or the other. He had moved with his force of 2000 men to Newcastle-under-Lyme, six miles from Blore Heath, and there waited on the turn of events, later commenting to his father-in-law that he regretted not having been able to be with him at the battle and hoped he could be of service at a later time.[18] On the other hand William, with nothing to lose and the example of his grandfather before him, set out to seek his fortune.

It is clear that even at this early stage, of what we now call the Wars of the Roses, Thomas was determined to maintain and keep the power, position and lands that he had recently inherited, and in this he was remarkably successful. William had no such incentives; as a younger son he had to make his own way in the world. The same choices seem to have applied in the fifteenth century as they did in the eighteenth, when for a second son it was either the army or the church.

For one who appears to have been ambitious the army would be the logical choice. The first Sir John had prospered through war and making a good marriage which turned into an even better one when his wife inherited her family's estates; with this as an example it would seem only natural to William to go to the wars when a war appeared. Although he had recently acquired the manor of Ridley in south Cheshire it is probable that his closest associations were with Lancashire and it is more likely that Lancashire men rather than Cheshire men formed the troops that he took to Blore Heath.[19] He joined Salisbury's army, and his presence during the battle together with his force of men dressed in Sir Thomas's livery helped to win the day.[20]

Although this second battle of the civil war was won by the Yorkist side the Lancastrians regrouped and the Yorkists were routed in a skirmish at Ludford Bridge outside Ludlow on 13 October. The Duke of York, his sons Edward, Earl of March, and Edmund, Earl of Rutland, together with the Neville Earls of Salisbury and Warwick fled. York and Rutland went to Ireland, March and the Nevilles to Calais via Devon.[21]

King Henry, now firmly back on the throne, summoned a Parliament to meet at Coventry in November. This Parliament "was perhaps the most packed, irregularly elected and stringently controlled of the century."[22] At this Parliament Sir Thomas Stanley was accused of failing to bring his troops to the king's side, but he successfully convinced it that he had been unable to reach the field of battle in time, despite the presence of his brother, with troops, on the Yorkist side. William, however, was not so lucky. On 14 October a commission was issued to Sir Richard Wellys to confiscate all the lands and possessions in Lincolnshire of Richard Duke of York, Richard Earl of Warwick, Richard Earl of Salisbury and, among others, *"William Stanley esquire,"* who were *"traitors and rebels."* [23] This Parliament also attainted them for treason, for in March 1460 Thomas Thorpe was appointed to receive all the possessions of those attainted for *"high treason in the parliament held last at Coventry"* and one of those mentioned is William Stanley.[24]

It is not known where William was at this time. It is possible that he went abroad to Calais with the Nevilles and the Earl of March,[25] although it may be that he hid successfully in the outer-lying regions of Lancashire or the Isle of Man. As the brother of one whose loyalty and support in the north the king was relying on, perhaps he was not pursued with vigour. Thomas had made his peace with the king, and it is probable that William kept his head down and waited on events.

He did not have to wait long.

The Earl of Warwick left Calais for Ireland in March 1460 and met the Duke of York at Waterford where they concerted their plans. Warwick landed with the Earl of March at Sandwich at the end of June and on 2 July 1460 entered

London.[26] On 3 July he addressed a meeting of Convocation at St Paul's and *"recited the cause of their coming into the land, how they had been put forth from the king's presence with great violence; so that they might never come to his presence to excuse themselves of the accusations laid against them."* [27] On 10 July the Yorkists won a decisive victory at Northampton and King Henry was taken prisoner. When the news of the defeat at Northampton reached Queen Margaret at Eccleshall Castle she fled to Chester with her son. While they were there an attempt was made to abduct her by a servant of Thomas Stanley.[28] This servant is named as John Cleger in the *Annales* of William of Worcester.[29] Parliament was summoned in the king's name to meet at Westminster on 7 October 1460. George Neville, Bishop of Exeter and Warwick's younger brother, was made Chancellor.

At this Parliament York made it plain that he intended to claim the throne, but Parliament was not ready to agree. After long debate the Lords agreed on 10 October by an Act of Settlement that, while Henry should keep his throne, York should be his heir and take the title Prince of Wales (thus disinheriting Henry's son Edward, who was now five years old). The delay caused by the argument gave the Lancastrians the opportunity to regroup, and on 30 December 1460 at the Battle of Wakefield the Yorkists suffered their worst defeat when both York and his son the Earl of Rutland were slain, their heads later being placed on Micklegate Bar in York.

On 2 February 1461 the Yorkists defeated the Lancastrians at the Battle of Mortimer's Cross, and again fought them at the Second Battle of St Albans on 17 February. The Earl of March was determined to avenge the death of his father. This he finally succeeded in doing on 29 March 1461 (Palm Sunday) at the Battle of Towton, near Tadcaster between York and Leeds.

Although the Earl of March was proclaimed King as Edward IV on 4 March 1461 both at St Paul's Cross and in Westminster Hall it was the Battle of Towton which made his throne secure.[30]

WHERE was William Stanley during this period? There is no indication whatever of his activities, but it is reasonable to suppose that at some point he joined either the Duke of York in Ireland (the Stanleys had strong Irish connections), or Warwick and March in Calais.

The descriptions of the Battle of Wakefield[31] make it highly unlikely that Sir William had joined the Duke of York, thus making it probable that he joined the Earl of March. He may also have been present at the Battles of Northampton, Mortimer's Cross and Towton, though there is no evidence that men from the Stanley estates were there.[32] However, it was after the Battle of Towton that a large number of nobles and knights, including Sir William Stanley, received their advancement, which may indicate that Sir William fought at the battle, although his reward could have been for his earlier support at Blore Heath.[33]

NOTES

1   Much of the early part of this chapter appeared in the author's articles in Blanc Sanglier (the magazine of the Yorkshire Branch of the Richard III Society) under the name Jean M. Perkins. For full citations of all books and articles referred to in this and other Chapters please see Bibliography.
2   Irvine, pp.47 and 52.
3   Seacome, p.16.
4   Irvine, p.55.
5   Bagley, p.5; Coward, p.4.
6   Coward, pp.5-6.
7   Irvine, p.57.
8   Bagley, p.6.
9   Bagley, pp.6-7.
10 Clayton, pp.76-77.
11 Family tree supplied by the late Pauline Routh.
12 Bagley, pp.7-8.
13 Clayton, p.89.
14 Clayton, p.77.
15 Hampton, p.28.
16 Clayton, p.77.
17 DNB entry for Sir William Stanley.
18 Bagley, p.9.
19 Clayton, p.81.
20 Clayton, p.79.
21 Kendall, Warwick, p.54.
22 Green, p.332.
23 CPR, Henry VI, vol.6 (1451-1461), p.561.
24 Ibid, p.572.
25 DNB entry for Sir William Stanley.
26 Cole, pp.75-76.
27 Green, p.334.
28 Cole, p.91.
29 Evans, p.152. Ch.6 note 2.
30 Cole, p.101.
31 Dockray, pp.238-56.
32 Clayton, p.91.
33 Boardman, p.52.

The Font in St. Chad's Church, Holt. The North West face showing at the top a badly damaged carving of the Trinity, below a human bust with flowing hair, and at the bottom a boar the emblem of Richard III.

Chapter Two

Edward IV - Advancement

FOR THE ambitious young William Stanley the decisive victory of the Yorkist cause at Towton was the start of an impressive career. Edward IV was on the throne, and the Lancastrian factions were either scattered, dead or captured, though not completely destroyed.

From Towton Edward IV went to York and there celebrated Easter. He was crowned at Westminster on Sunday 28 June 1461,[1] at the age of nineteen.

After the Battle of Towton the Stanleys began to consolidate their position in the north-west of England. It would appear that the support that Sir William had given the Yorkist cause resulted in almost immediate benefits for the family. Thomas was granted the offices that had been held by his father, now that the Lancastrian holders of those offices had fled. Thomas was also made Receiver for the Duchy of Lancaster in 1461. He was included in the emergency commission of Justices for Cheshire held on 26 May 1461 and this was followed on 1 January 1462 by his appointment as Justice for life, a position he held until his death in 1504 except for a brief period in 1471.

It was important to the King to appoint trustworthy and efficient men to high office. The appointment of men of lesser rank to the positions of Sheriff and Justice of the Peace often led to corruption and inefficiency.[2]

Edward IV knighted William Stanley on 27 June 1461[3] and also rewarded him with grants of lands, offices and honours, particularly in the region of Cheshire and North Wales. On 1 May 1461 he was appointed Chamberlain of Chester for life[4] and was also granted, at the supplication of the king's sister Anne Duchess of Exeter the lordships of Hope and Hopesdale in Flintshire, Manorbere in Pembrokeshire, Northwich and Overmershe in Cheshire, Newton and Haydock in Lancashire, and Dalbere, Dalberelees and Wyrkesworth in Derbyshire *"to hold for her use for her life."*[5] This grant was confirmed on 16 July 1461, when William Stanley was referred to as "knight," whereas in the earlier grant he was designated "esquire." On 16 September 1462 he was granted *"all lands called 'Cobbeshole' co. Kent belonging lately to Robert Myrfyn, a rebel, valued at £100 per year."* In this grant he is described as one of the King's "Kervers" or "carvers."[6]

The first major grant to Sir William was made on 1 February 1462 when King Edward granted him:

"the Castle, manor and lordship of Skipton in Craven, co.York, with all the towns hamlets lands rents services reversions advowsons fees offices franchises mines of coal and lead and other possessions lately belonging to John late Lord Clifford on 29 March [1461] and in the king's hands by reason of an Act of Forfeiture in Parliament at Westminster 4 November."[7]

This grant may have particular significance because of the later relationship between the house of Clifford and Sir William Stanley. The grant did not go down well with Roger and Robert, the surviving brothers of John Clifford, who lived to be implacable enemies to the Yorkist cause.

This grant of Skipton was confirmed on 29 May 1464, and added: *"all waifs strays forfeitures, goods and chattels of felons fugitives and outlaws, deodands and treasure trove, free warren and free chase, and return of writs and executions."* [8]

In December 1462 both Sir William and his brother Thomas Stanley marched with Edward IV and the Earl of Warwick against the Scots. They had raised an army of 400 archers (probably Cheshire men noted for their archery skills) to fight for Edward. The Stanley brothers were given the task of laying siege to Alnwick Castle, which was being held by Queen Margaret and used by her as a base from which to ravage the northern counties. The siege began on or shortly after 10 December 1462. This period is one of great civil unrest, showing that Edward's crown was not secure. In February 1463 Sir William had to leave the occupation of Alnwick, which had capitulated on 6 January 1463,[9] to return to Cheshire to *"arrest all persons in Cheshire who in disobedience to the proclamation had failed to join the king in his expedition to Scotland."* [10] This Sir William was successful in doing.

In 1464 there was again trouble, when the Lancastrian Duke of Somerset, whom Edward had tried to draw into his own fold,[11] revolted, and Jasper Tudor stirred up trouble in Wales. These disturbances were put down by the Stanleys. King Henry had disappeared after the Battle of Hexham in May and had wandered south, staying at one loyal refuge after another until he reached Waddington in Lancashire, the home of Sir Richard Tempest, where he was betrayed to the Yorkists, possibly by his host's brother. Henry was taken under guard to London and lodged in the Tower on 14 July 1465.[12] Following Henry's discovery at Waddington Queen Margaret escaped to France.[13] It was becoming apparent that there would be no peace in the realm until the Lancastrian threat had been eliminated.

On 12 November 1465 the grant of Skipton was extended to *"William Stanley, knight, and Joan Lovell late the wife of John Lovell, knight, Lord Lovell, whom he will shortly marry, and the heirs male of his body."* [14] Sir William must have been secure enough of his position to look for a wife. By marrying Joan Lovell, a widow and heiress, he gained control of both her inherited estates and those of her son during his minority. When she died in the following August he lost these advantages and had to retreat back to his original stamping ground.[15]

On 16 September 1464 Sir William was appointed Clerk and Prothonotary of the Justice of Chester.[16] He was appointed Sheriff of the County of Chester for life on 26 February 1466.[17] In 1467 he was made Steward of Bromfield and Yale under two co-owners of the lordship, Lord Abergavenny and the Duke of Norfolk, who appointed him commissioner and councillor.[18] Having proved himself both loyal and efficient, on 29 September 1469 he was appointed Constable of Rhuddlan, Caernarfon and Beaumaris castles for life, thus extending his influence well into North Wales. This was followed on 14 February 1470 by his being appointed Steward of Denbigh for life.[19]

It was now that civil war broke out in earnest.

From the autumn of 1463 the Earl of Warwick had been trying to negotiate a marriage between Edward and Anne, daughter of the King of France, and so was surprised and shocked to discover that Edward had secretly married a Lancastrian widow, Elizabeth Woodville, who already had two sons, some five months prior to his admission of the fact on 14 September 1464 at a meeting of the Great Council.[20] Warwick felt betrayed by his king, who had allowed him to continue negotiations with the French when he had had no intention of complying with any agreement.

It was over the next few years that Warwick's disillusionment grew and he began secretly to oppose the King. He planned to marry his daughter Isabel to George, Duke of Clarence, the King's brother and heir. This did not please Edward. However, Clarence went to Calais and there married Isabel on Tuesday 11 July 1469. He then joined Warwick in signing a manifesto calling on all true subjects to join them at Canterbury on 16 July to present a petition to the King denouncing the Woodvilles and their friends.

They landed in Kent and marched through London to join with an army from the north gathered by "Robin of Redesdale." A battle was fought at Edgecote on 26 July 1469 and the King's army was defeated in his absence. The news reached Edward on 29 July after he had left Nottingham. His army now melted away and he was taken prisoner by the Earl of Warwick and incarcerated at Warwick Castle. The Queen's father and brother, Earl Rivers and Sir John Woodville, were caught and executed.[21]

Edward was subsequently moved for safety to Middleham Castle, Warwick's stronghold, to prevent a southern attempt to release him. While at Middleham there appears to have been an attempt to rescue him. The chronicle relates a rumour that,

"Now on a daie, upon a plaine, when he was thus abrode, there met with him Sir William Stanleie, Sir Thomas a Borough, and divers other of his friends, with such a great band of men, that neither his keepers would, nor once durst, move him to return unto prison againe. Some have thought that his keepers were corrupted with monie, or faire promises, and therefore suffered him thus to scape out of danger." [22]

However as Edward was subsequently brought to York from Middleham on 29 September by Warwick this "escape" cannot have taken place. It is of interest, though, that Sir William Stanley is reported to have been involved in the plot as it illustrates the perception of his loyalty to the Yorkist cause. Edward was taken to Pontefract after leaving York, and because of the rebellion which broke out on the Scottish borders, led by those wishing to reinstate Henry, Warwick released him in order that this threat could be overcome.[23]

On 25 July 1470 Edward Prince of Wales, son of Henry VI, was betrothed to Warwick's daughter Lady Anne Neville at Angers in France. On 9 September Warwick set sail from France with his brother-in-law the Earl of Oxford and Jasper Tudor, Earl of Pembroke. Four days later he landed at Dartmouth and proclaimed Henry VI as king. Edward IV had been drawn north but because the Earl of Worcester's cruelty had alienated people from him he was unable to acquire a force to attack his enemies, and fled to Burgundy via King's Lynn. The news of the king's flight reached London on 1 October and Queen Elizabeth and her children took sanctuary in Westminster Abbey.

On 6 October Warwick entered London and went to the Tower to kneel at Henry's feet. Henry was then taken in state to the Bishop of London's palace. The following week, on 13 October, Henry was taken to the Palace of Westminster to be crowned again and to be installed in the royal apartments. Thomas Stanley had joined with Warwick and was present when Henry was taken to Westminster to be crowned.[24] Thus at this point he had thrown in his lot with the Lancastrian faction. He must have felt that this revolt and overthrow of Edward was going to mean a permanent restoration or re-adeption of Henry, as Thomas is notorious for staying well away from intrigue and commitment to either cause.

While in sanctuary Queen Elizabeth gave birth on 1 November 1470 to a son, named Edward after his father.[25] Anne Neville married Edward Prince of Wales at Amboise on 13 December 1470.

Meanwhile Sir William Stanley had remained loyal to King Edward, and he suffered for it. On 29 September 1470 about four hundred armed Nantwich men attacked Sir William as Chamberlain of Chester, shooting at him with arrows and howling, *"A Warwick! A Warwick! King Henry! Prince Edward!"* Sir William and two friends were beaten and robbed. Sir William was called a traitor and jailed along with John Conway and John ap Ellis. He lost over a thousand pounds in jewels, horses and arms in the robbery, and had to pay ten marks in ransom to get out of prison.[26] This attack on Sir William Stanley could have been a result of the rumours of the previous summer when Sir William was implicated in helping Edward escape from Middleham Castle. It would appear that the importance of rumour at this time should not be underestimated.

Edward's Return

ON 11 March 1471 Edward, with eighteen ships hired from Charles of Burgundy and £400 borrowed from wool merchants against the preservation of the wool trade with England, set sail from Flushing. He had an army of about 1,500 men including 300 Flemings with handguns. He had planned to land at Cromer in Norfolk, but hearing that the Earl of Oxford was heading in that direction sailed north and landed on the north bank of the Humber. His welcome was far from cordial and the gates of Kingston-upon-Hull were closed against him. However, Edward was not slow to assess the public mood and gave out that he had only come to reclaim the duchy of York, and loudly proclaiming his allegiance to Henry VI he set off towards York. At York he was met with hostility but managed to charm his way into the city and for the gates to be opened to his army. The next day he marched to Tadcaster and then to Wakefield and Doncaster. In doing so he evaded the Lancastrian force of the Earl of Oxford, who had brought his East Anglian troops to Pontefract. Edward moved south to Nottingham, where Sir William Stanley and Sir William Norris joined him with a force of 300 men from Lord Hastings' affinity.[27] As he moved towards his enemy it moved back before him until he reached Coventry where he invited the Earl of Warwick to meet him. At this point George Duke of Clarence took his army over to his brother, and they met on the Banbury road on 3 April 1471. Edward then continued on his way to London.

London was in confusion, not knowing which king to support, but finally they welcomed Edward, and King Henry, who had greeted him warmly, was sent back to the Tower. On Good Friday, 12 April 1471, Edward marshalled his forces and set out to meet Warwick's army before it could join up with that of Queen Margaret and other Lancastrians coming from the south. Edward took King Henry with him as prisoner so that he should not fall into Lancastrian hands, and the two armies met at Barnet on 14 April, Easter Sunday. The battle was confused and bloody. During it King Henry managed to escape, but was recaptured halfway to St Albans. The Earl of Warwick and his brother Montague were slain, together with 1,500 others, and it was still only eight o'clock in the morning.

Queen Margaret landed at Weymouth on Easter Sunday but the news did not reach London until Tuesday. The populace wanted peace and chose Edward to give it to them. They voted him 1000 marks and prayed him to deliver them. The Duke of Somerset and the Earl of Devon, however, joined Queen Margaret. Edward mustered his troops at Windsor, where he celebrated St George's day, and on 24 April he set out westward. Queen Margaret's strategy was brilliant. She completely misled Edward as to her intentions and he had to pursue her towards the Severn. The Lancastrians made for Gloucester but the gates were closed against them, and with Edward now close behind they were caught between two fires. To avoid being trapped they turned for Tewkesbury where there was a ferry across the Severn. As Edward was too close for her army to cross before he arrived Margaret turned to fight, to gain time for the crossing.[28]

The next day was Saturday 4 May 1471, and at dawn the Lancastrian army prepared for an attack from King Edward's forces. Among those present on the King's side was Sir William Stanley. On the Lancastrian side Edward Prince of Wales was to lead the main battle. After taking leave of her son, Queen Margaret went with a number of her ladies to a small religious house at Gupshill. The Duke of Gloucester commanded the Yorkists' vanguard and the artillery, King Edward the centre, and Lords Hastings and Dorset the rear. The battle did not last long. The Lancastrians broke and ran before the Yorkist onslaught and fled in all directions. It was short and bloody with a great slaughter on "Bloody Meadow." The Prince of Wales had borne himself valiantly but was carried away in the rout and was slain between Gastons and Tewkesbury. He was seventeen years old. His body was buried in the Abbey church at Tewkesbury.[29] The king conferred knighthood on forty-three officers including Sir William Stanley, thus making him a knight banneret.[30]

Queen Margaret and her ladies escaped across the Avon and took refuge at Payne's Place, and the next day fled for safety towards Worcester. There they were captured by Sir William Stanley, who announced with callous brutality the death of Prince Edward. Sir William then escorted Queen Margaret to Edward IV at Coventry on 11 May 1461, and from there she was taken to London and lodged in the Tower. She remained in custody until a ransom was paid in 1475, then left England and lived in Anjou until her death in 1482.[31]

The Yorkist victory at Tewkesbury heralded a period of peace and stability which had not been known in the kingdom for nearly twenty years.

Sir William Stanley's reward for his support was twofold. Firstly he married Elizabeth Hopton,[32] the widow of John Tiptoft, Earl of Worcester (executed in 1470), and secondly he gained, on 7 December 1471,

> *"the custody of all castles, lordships, manors, lands, rents, services and other possessions with knight's fees and advow-sons late of the said John* [Tiptoft] *during the minority of Edward his son and heir and the custody and marriage of the latter without dis-paragement..."* [33]

The young Earl of Worcester had been born on 14 July 1469, thus giving Sir William and his wife many years in charge of this inheritance.[34]

In 1472, shortly after the death of her second husband Henry Stafford, Thomas Stanley married Lady Margaret Beaufort, daughter of John Duke of Somerset who died in 1444. Her first husband was Edmund Tudor Earl of Richmond, by whom she had one son, her only child, Henry Tudor. She was descended from John of Gaunt Duke of Lancaster, by his relationship with Katherine Swynford whom he later married. The children of this relationship were legitimized by Henry IV but he excluded a right to the throne. Henry Tudor had been brought up in the household of William Herbert, Earl of Pembroke, and had taken part in Warwick's rebellion, but had fled to France after the Battle of Edgecote on 24 July 1469. Lady Margaret attempted to improve her son's prospects by asking the king continually to bring him to court. However, his association with Herbert and Henry VI and his flight to France made this more unlikely. Her marriage to Thomas Stanley can be seen as a search for allies in this cause.[35] Her attempts to bring her son back to England culminated on 3 June 1482 in a document in which Edward stated that Henry might be allowed to return.[36] However he did not arrive before King Edward's death in 1483.

The first Parliament after the restoration of Edward IV had voted money to pay for a war against France, but by 1474 the expedition had not set out, and as Parliament was reluctant to vote more money Edward had to resort to extorting "benevolences." These were forced loans which made the king unpopular.[37] As part of Edward's attempt to manage his finances he passed ordinances to regulate his household management and expenses.[38] Edward IV also increased his control over the customs service in order to stop the evasion of customs duties.[39] As part of this, Sir William Stanley and Thomas Lord Stanley were among those appointed on 3 August 1474 to a commission set up to enquire into the whereabouts of shipments of wool and hides which were in various ports in England instead of in Calais.[40]

The next important event for Sir William came on 5 March 1475 when his lordship of Skipton-in-Craven, which had been granted to him in 1465, was now exchanged for *"the castle, lordship and manor of Chirk and Chirkland in the Marches of Wales adjoining the county of Salop, and the lordship and manor of Wilmyngton, co. Kent..."*[41] While this reduced the area of Sir William's sphere of influence it greatly enhanced his hold on the Welsh Marches and southern Cheshire.

Some of Sir Williams duties were military. On 21 August 1474 a commission was set up under Sir William and others *"to take muster of the king's knight Gilbert Debenham and 400 archers in his company, whom the king ordered to be sent to Ireland, in any place near the city of Chester on 9 September next or within three days following and to certify them to the king and council."*[42] On 23 April 1475 Sir William again headed a commission of Cheshire men set up to arrest a group of men who had taken *"the king's wages from Gilbert Debenham to serve the king in Ireland... but had not yet come to the king's service, and to imprison them until they shall restore the said wages or find security that they will serve the king..."*[43] This was in response to their failure to turn up the previous Agust. Later on, in August 1478, Sir William Stanley and others were ordered to take muster near Conway of 300 men at arms and archers *"whom the king has ordered to Ireland with Henry Gray..."*[44]

Both Stanley brothers joined Edward IV's expedition to France.[45] In 1475 Edward at last managed to put together an alliance with Charles, Duke of Burgundy, and set out on his expedition to France in June 1475. This was not destined to be the military exploit with the promise of spoil and booty that many had hoped for. Louis XI was determined not to lose a major battle and therefore offered Edward 75,000 crowns down and 50,000 crowns per annum for life, and another 50,000 as ransom for Margaret of Anjou. Edward was only too happy to accept and by 28 September he and his army were back in London.[46]

On 26 June 1475 the king granted to *"William Stanley, knight of the body, and the heirs male of his body, the manors of Hornemede, in Hornmede, co. Hertford, and Enhalle, co. Cambridge"* and various messuages and tenements in Suffolk, and the manor and lordship of Flete by Sandwich, co. Kent.[47]

Thomas Lord Stanley was appointed Steward of the Household in 1471 after the restoration of Edward IV, which shows that he had managed to avoid being penalized for his "treasonable" support of the Earl of Warwick. He held the position until 1483.[48] His standing was such that he was one of those lords who in July 1476 escorted the remains of Richard Duke of York and the Earl of Rutland from their graves at Pontefract Priory to tnew tombs at Fotheringhay.[49]

Sir Thomas also played an important role as Receiver of the Duchy of Lancaster when King Edward made his progress through his Duchy lands in August and September 1487. There was an enquiry into the efficient collection of the Duchy revenues, and because of the enforcements ordered by the king he was able to improve the revenues, from £347.3s.1¼d in 1476-77 to £885.3s. 1³⁄₄d in 1480-81[50]

At some point during this period Sir William Stanley was appointed to the household of the Prince of Wales at Ludlow. He is given as *"stuard of his* [the Prince of Wales'] *houshould."*[51] This appointment would have great significance after the death of the king.

As part of his judicial duties Sir William was among others on a commission of Oyer and Terminer in March 1483, to inquire into *"certain treasons, felonies, trespasses and other offences committed by John Kent and William Clyfton in the county of Hereford and the marches of Wales adjacent,"* thus showing that firm control over the Welsh border area was essential.[52] Sir William had also been appointed to the Council of the Welsh Marches, which was headed by the Duke of Gloucester.

NOTES

1   Cole, p.109.
2   Lander (2), p.14.
3   Williams, J., p.118.
4   Clayton, p.93.

5   CPR Edward IV, 1461-67, p.7.
6   CPR Edward IV, 1461-67, p.198. A "king's carver" was the position of a king's knight and was a household appointment. (See Myers (1), p.249, n.97.)
7   CPR Edward IV, 1461-67, p.115.
8   CPR Edward IV, 1461-67, p.342.
9   Hicks, p.23.
10 McKelvey, p.77.
11 Hicks, pp.24-25.
12 Cole, pp.131-33.
13 McKelvey, p.78.
14 CPR Edward IV, 1461-67, p.474.
15 The wives and children of Sir William Stanley will be dealt with in Chapter Eight, below.
16 Clayton, p.167.
17 Ibid.
18 Jones (1), p.11.
19 Clayton, p.167.
20 Cole, p.128.
21 Cole, pp.141-45.
22 Hollinshed, p.134.
23 Lander (2), p.119.
24 Clayton, p.103.
25 Clayton, p.109.
26 McKelvey, p.152.
27 Clayton, p.109.
28 Cole, pp.152-62.
29 Markham, pp.73-76.
30 Wheeler, p.20.
31 Markham, pp.78-79.
32 The wives and children of Sir William Stanley will be dealt with in Chapter Eight, below.
33 CPR Edward IV, 1467-77, p.297.
34 Cokayne, vol.12, p.845.
35 Jones and Underwood, pp.35-61.
36 Gill, p.64.
37 Chrimes (3), p.117.
38 Myers (1).
39 Lander (2), p.20.
40 CPR Edward IV, 1467-77, p.491; Clayton, p.167.
41 CPR Edward IV, 1467-77, p.505.
42 CPR Edward IV, 1467-77, p.491.
43 CPR Edward IV, 1467-77, p.497.
44 CPR Edward IV, 1476-85, p.121.
45 Clayton, p.112
46 Chrimes (3), p.118.
47 CPR Edward IV, 1467-77, p.556.
48 Myers (1), p.287.
49 Hammond (3).
50 Myers (2), p.7, n.24.
51 Nicols, pp.vii-viii.
52 CPR Edward IV, 1476-85, p.345.

Chapter Three

Richard III - Disillusionment

EDWARD IV died unexpectedly on 9 April 1483, catching all the chief players in the realm in the wrong place.

His heir, his twelve-year-old son Edward Prince of Wales, now King Edward V, was with his own court at Ludlow under the care of his uncle Anthony Earl Rivers. This court consisted of, among others, his half-brother Richard Grey, Sir Thomas Vaughan his Chamberlain, and Sir William Stanley the Steward of his household.[1] Richard Duke of Gloucester was in Yorkshire at his castle at Middleham, where the news of the king's death did not reach him until about 15 April.[2]

On his death-bed Edward had made provision for the future by entrusting the realm to his brother Richard as Protector instead of to his queen and her family as regents. He remembered only too well the problems caused by the minority of Henry VI and was determined that faction should not mar his son's accession. He knew that Richard could command the obedience of the older nobility which despised the queen and her relatives, and before he died he managed to arrange a reconciliation between Lord Hastings and his stepson Thomas Grey, Marquess of Dorset.[3]

Preparations for King Edward's funeral began at once, and it was over before the arrival of the new king or his uncle Richard Duke of Gloucester. In the days following the king's death his body was embalmed, and on Wednesday 17 April it was taken to Westminster Abbey attended by members of his household including Sir Edward Stanley, son of Sir Thomas. Sir Thomas himself attended as Steward of the Household. After the funeral Mass at Westminster the coffin and procession set out for Windsor, stopping at Syon for the night. The cortège arrived at Windsor on the evening of 18 April and the burial itself took place on the following day with Sir Thomas attending.[4]

However, once King Edward was dead the Woodville faction moved to circumvent the king's wishes, by taking advantage of their slender majority in the Council to pass a resolution that Richard's Protectorship should be replaced by a regency council headed, but not dominated by, the Duke of Gloucester.

To give this move a stamp of legality they also proposed to bring the king to Westminster for his coronation as soon as possible. This would immediately bring to an end any Protectorate or regency council, as on his coronation the king would legally attain his majority and thus be free to choose his own advisors. They further proposed that Earl Rivers should bring with the new king as many armed men as he could muster on the road from Ludlow. This move antagonised even members of the queen's party, and Lord Hastings threatened to withdraw to Calais, thus exposing the divisions within the Council. Hastings had been keeping Richard fully informed of the events in London and urged him to make haste with an army to reach London before Rivers arrived from Ludlow. Richard held a funeral service for his brother in York and took an oath of fealty to the new king, and news of these actions won him the support of several of the waverers in London. However, the Council, including Sir Thomas Stanley, decided that the date of the coronation would be 4 May, and Rivers was instructed to make sure that the king arrived in London no later than 1 May.

It was shortly after Edward IV was buried at Windsor on 19 April that Richard left York for Northampton with a retinue of about 600 men. At Northampton he was to join Rivers and the king to progress together to London. There is no record of whether or not Sir William Stanley was with the retinue from Ludlow. It is, however, most likely that he would seek to attend the new king, as a member of his household, and even aspire to retain his post of Steward of the Household with the new king, even though his brother held the post of Steward of the Household to Edward IV. Gloucester arrived at Northampton on 29 April, to discover that the king's retinue had already passed through the town and was staying the night at Stony Stratford.

During the evening Earl Rivers rode back to Northampton, presented the king's greetings to his uncle, and explained that they had continued to Stony Stratford because the town of Northampton was too small to contain both retinues. Richard invited him to stay for supper.

During the meal the Duke of Buckingham arrived. It could be that this meeting was pre-arranged, but after Rivers had retired to bed they held a conference at which it is thought that Buckingham pointed out to Richard that if the king was crowned the rôle of Protector would end and the Woodville faction would achieve power. It must also have been apparent that with the small number of men they had available, if they wished to act they must do so at once.

At dawn on 30 April Richard ordered the arrest of Rivers and then rode to Stony Stratford to meet the king. After offering his condolences on the death of his father, Richard then took charge of the king's person and arrested Richard Grey and Sir Thomas Vaughan, the Prince's Chamberlain. The king's Welsh escort was told to go home.

When the news reached London the queen took sanctuary in Westminster Abbey together with her other children. The Marquess of Dorset, failing to raise a force to "rescue" the king, joined the queen in sanctuary. Public opinion was on the side of Richard. Lord Hastings, still in London, did his best to calm the situation by calling a meeting of the remaining lords at St Paul's and explaining that the Duke of Gloucester was faithful to the king, and that Lords Rivers and Grey were arrested for attempts against the Dukes of Gloucester and Buckingham. A letter arrived from Richard promising an early coronation.

The king and the two dukes made their entry into London on 4 May and made their way to the Bishop of London's Palace at St Paul's, where the king was lodged. On the same day the lords, bishops, Mayor and aldermen were invited to take the oath of allegiance. The coronation was set to take place on 24 June, and on the following day the Lords and Commons would be asked to ratify the Protectorate. At Buckingham's suggestion the king was moved to the royal apartments in the Tower,[5] where he was joined by his brother the Duke of York on 16 June.[6]

The king's Council was largely unchanged from that of Edward IV except for those lords who had been arrested by Richard. However, he had not replaced them by others who would be his own supporters, and the Council was weighted against him if there were any dissent. It was after 5 June that the new crisis erupted. Richard had discovered that four members of the Council had begun to meet informally to discuss the situation. These four were Lord Hastings, Thomas Lord Stanley, and the Bishops Rotherham and Morton, who were meeting at the Tower while Richard's intimates gathered at Crosby Place, his residence. This in itself was not too significant until Richard heard that Hastings was beginning to have contact with the queen, who was still in sanctuary at Westminster.

It would appear that Hastings' about-face was caused by his fear of losing his power to Buckingham, who now appeared to have taken over the role of "kingmaker." Hastings had been Lord Chamberlain to Edward IV and had retained the position under Edward V, and he could have hoped to continue after the coronation, but he now found that Richard intended to extend his own authority until the king came of age.[7]

Richard took steps to remove this nest of opposition, probably on 13 June (though there is some doubt about this date as some authorities give 20 June.[8]) While the Council was in session at Westminster Richard summoned the four offenders, together with Buckingham, Howard and a number of members of his personal staff, to a meeting in the Tower. What happened next has been described by Sir Thomas More who, it is believed, got his information from Bishop Morton. This would, of course, have given his story a bias against Richard, but it is one that has persisted as truth for over five hundred years. On entering the council chamber as though he had just heard some disturbing news Richard asked what should be done to those who threatened the Protector and the king. Hastings replied that they should be punished as traitors, whoever they were. Richard answered that it was the queen and her family. Hastings responded that they should still be punished, if they were traitors. At this, someone cried "Treason!" and armed men rushed into the room and arrested Hastings, Stanley, Rotherham and Morton. Hastings was allowed a chaplain to make his peace with God and he was summarily executed on Tower Green.[9]

When the armed men entered a fight broke out and Thomas Stanley was struck on the head and wounded. This did not prevent his being imprisoned in the

Tower.[10] But he had been released by the time of Richard's coronation and in fact was restored to the Council almost immediately.[11] Therefore the only person who received the ultimate punishment for treason was Hastings.

There now followed what is usually described as "the usurpation of Richard III." This took the form of declaring Edward IV's marriage to Elizabeth Woodville illegal on the grounds that he had been pre-contracted to Lady Eleanor Butler and was therefore not free to marry, and that the children of this illegal marriage were bastards and could not succeed to the throne. This meant that as Richard himself was the only heir of his brother he was himself king. A sermon to this effect was preached at St Paul's Cross by the Prebendary of St Paul's Cathedral, Dr Ralph Shaa, on 22 June. Ralph Shaa was a brother of Edmund Shaa, Lord Mayor of London at that time.[12]

On 24 June Buckingham enlarged on this theme and when a Parliament of the Lords and Commons met at Westminster on Wednesday 25 June it did not oppose the idea of Richard becoming king. They put into their petition, known as "Titulus Regius," the reasons for believing that Richard was the only true king, and presented it to Richard begging him to take the throne.[13] This he agreed to do, apparently reluctantly, and then rode in state to Westminster Hall and laid formal claim to his title by seating himself on the marble chair of King's Bench. [14] He subsequently dated his reign from 26 June 1483. Sir William Stanley is said to have been present at Westminster Hall when Richard took his seat.[15]

At some time following this the princes, now both lodged in the Tower, began to be seen less and less frequently until finally they were not seen at all.[16]

Meanwhile, in Yorkshire the Earl of Northumberland and Sir Richard Ratcliffe supervised the execution of Anthony Earl Rivers, Richard Grey and Sir Thomas Vaughan at Pontefract.[17]

On 6 July 1483 Richard and his wife Anne were crowned at Westminster Abbey. Lord Stanley carried the Steward's mace, though after this Thomas Howard, Earl of Surrey, was appointed Steward.[18] Sir William Stanley also appears in the list of those attending.[19]

RICHARD was now on the throne and was *de facto* king, but his position was not secure, as later developments were to prove, although at this time both Thomas and William Stanley, however reluctantly, had sided with Richard's party. Any doubt they felt could have had its origins in their relationships with Edward IV and the young Edward V. These feelings could have been worked upon to lead them to support Henry Tudor, Earl of Richmond, in the future.

Two weeks after his coronation Richard set out on a royal progress through the West Country, the Midlands, Yorkshire and the north. First he rewarded the Duke of Buckingham by appointing him Constable and Great Chamberlain of England, and recognised his claim to the Bohun inheritance; he rewarded the Earl of Northumberland by granting him the Wardenship of the West March, and the Palatinate in Cumberland; and he granted John Howard, the newly created Duke of Norfolk, Crown lands worth £1000 a year in Suffolk, Essex, Kent and Cambridgeshire.[20] Because of Thomas Stanley's treachery there were no awards made to either of the Stanleys. On about 20 July the royal progress left Windsor. It proceeded in a stately way to York, where it was received on 29 August 1483, with Lord Stanley in the train,[21] and there on 7 September Richard's son Edward was invested as Prince of Wales in the Palace of the Archbishop of York.

Meanwhile powerful forces were conspiring against Richard in the south. Some time during late August and early September the princes were no longer seen in the Tower, and rumours of their death or disappearance led to an alliance between the Woodville faction, now dispossessed by the ascendance of Richard, and traditional Lancastrian supporters in the south. The Lancastrian claimant was now the twenty-six year old son of Margaret Beaufort and stepson of Sir Thomas Stanley, the Earl of Richmond, who had spent much of his life outside England and was little-known there.

The Duke of Buckingham, until this point a staunch supporter of Richard and an instigator of Richard's claim to the throne, now joined the rebellion against him. Initially the rebellion was to set Edward V on the throne, but when rumours of his death appeared the rebellion changed tack in favour of Henry Earl of Richmond. One of the leading figures in the move towards rebellion was Henry's mother Margaret Beaufort, Lady Stanley. Her husband was not involved.

Richard was in Lincoln on 11 October when he learnt that Buckingham had joined this conspiracy. Buckingham's rebellion makes no sense unless it is assumed that he was making his own bid for the throne from the beginning - he was descended from Thomas of Woodstock and had at least as good a claim to the throne as Henry Earl of Richmond. Henry, though, had promised to marry Elizabeth, the eldest daughter of Elizabeth Woodville and Edward IV, if he succeeded in taking the throne, which would have won him the support of the Woodville faction.

The weather and King Richard's information system managed to thwart the rebellion, and Buckingham was betrayed for the £1000 reward placed on his head. Hearing of the collapse of the rebellion Richmond returned to France to await a better opportunity. Buckingham, having been tried by the Vice-Constable, Sir Ralph Assheton, was beheaded on 2 November in Salisbury market place.[22] Henry swore a solemn oath in the cathedral of Rennes on Christmas Day 1483 that he would marry Elizabeth.

Richard returned to London on 25 November 1483.

His first and only Parliament met on 23 January 1484, and William Catesby was elected Speaker. Richard's title was confirmed, followed by the attainders. Ninety-five men singled out as leaders of the rebellion had their lands confiscated. The Duchess of Buckingham was granted an annuity, and Margaret Beaufort's land were placed in the keeping of her husband, Lord Stanley, who had remained loyal to Richard throughout the rebellion. On 20 February the Commons granted Richard the Customs revenues.[23] The Parliament also passed an Act freeing the king's subjects from the "benevolences" instituted by Edward IV.[24]

Richard's greatest source of power and wealth lay in the Crown lands and those of the attainted and dead Lancastrians. The confiscation which followed Buckingham's rebellion gave him additional property for redistribution to his supporters. Among those who received benefits were Thomas Stanley and his brother Sir William, on the Welsh Marches.[25]

On 10 December 1484 the grant of lands to Sir William Stanley was confirmed. These included *"the castle, town and lordship of Denasbrayn, the castle, town and lordship of Holt, the lordships manors and lands called Hewlyngton, Bromfeld, Yale, Wrexham, ... Ridley ..."* as well as various *"offices reversions services and hereditaments late of John, late duke of Norfolk and George Neville..."* [26]

Elizabeth Woodville and her five daughters came out of sanctuary in March 1484.[27]

With the renewed threat from Richmond, who was gathering troops and supporters in France, Richard prepared for war. He moved towards Nottingham on 20 March 1484 to set up a base from which he could mount a defence against any assault from whichever direction it should come. It was here, in the middle of April, that he received the news that his son Edward Prince of Wales had died at Middleham Castle.

This news gave the magnates pause for thought. Who was now the heir to the throne? At first Richard advanced Edward Earl of Warwick, the son of his brother George Duke of Clarence, who had been debarred from the throne by his father's attainder, but who was at least legitimate. He was taken to Sheriff Hutton Castle in Yorkshire where he was established with a household. Richard's final choice of heir was another nephew: John de la Pole, Earl of Lincoln, the eldest son of the Duke of Suffolk and Richard's sister Elizabeth. On 21 August 1484 Richard appointed Lincoln Lord Lieutenant of Ireland, an appointment usually held by the Yorkist heir apparent.[28]

In August Richard returned to London, and one of the things he found time to do was have the bones of Henry VI exhumed on 12 August 1484 and transferred from Chertsey to St George's Chapel at Windsor.[29] By 11 September he had returned to Nottingham, where he received the Scottish ambassadors in state. The embassy included the Earl of Argyll and the Bishop of Aberdeen. Among those present in the Great Hall of Nottingham Castle was Thomas Lord Stanley. In the ten days of negotiations a three-year truce was agreed which ruled out Scotland's giving aid to Richmond, thus closing a gateway into England. By this time of the year it was too late to expect an invasion. However, Richard did not return to the capital until 11 November.

Treason was in the air, and at Christmas Richard heard that the proposed invasion was to take place the following summer.

Early in March 1485 Queen Anne died of a wasting disease. Rumourmongers began to say that Richard had poisoned her and that he now planned to marry his niece Elizabeth. Despite his best efforts Richard could not dispel these rumours, which unsettled the population and played into the hands of Richmond.

In order to pay for the coming campaign Richard resorted to benevolences, which he had spoken against but was compelled to use as there was no time to call another Parliament to vote him the cash to repel the invaders.

On 2 June Richard put his commissioners of array on special alert, but he also knew that much depended on the loyalty of a few men in high places. One such man was Thomas Lord Stanley, who in July sought the king's permission to visit his family in Lancashire. Richard knew that this could influence others to withdraw, so proposed a compromise by which Stanley was allowed to go but had to send his son George Lord Strange to Nottingham in his place.

On 24 July news reached Richard that Richmond was making ready to embark at Harfleur.[30]

NOTES

1   Nichols, pp.vii-viii.
2   Gill, p.52.
3   Cheetham, p.102.
4   Sutton and Visser Fuchs, pp.372-73, 379.
5   Cheetham, pp.102-10.
6   Pollard, p.93.
7   Cheetham, pp.111-12.
8   Hanham, pp.821-27; Hammond (2), pp.10-12.
9   Cheetham, p.114.
10 Bagley, p.14.
11 Cheetham, p.117.
12 Blunden-Ellis, p.13.
13 Cheetham, pp.118-21; Kendall (1), pp.221-23.
14 Cheetham, p.123.
15 McKelvey, p.300.
16 Pollard, p.120.
17 Cheetham, p.123.
18 Myers (1), p.287.
19 Sutton and Hammond, pp.271, 280.
20 Cheetham, p.129.
21 Hammond (2), p.3.
22 Cheetham, pp.130-40.
23 Cheetham, pp.151-59.
24 Virgoe, p.25.
25 Cheetham, p.160.
26 CPR 1476-1485, p.516. This must refer to John Mowbray, Duke of Norfolk (died 1476) and George Neville, Duke of Bedford, son of John Neville, Marquess Montague.
27 Drewett and Redhead, p.141.
28 Cheetham, pp.163-66.
29 Ibid, p.168; White, p.76.
30 Cheetham, pp.168-79.

Chapter Four

The Battle of Bosworth

AT SOME point during the reign of Richard III the Stanleys, both Thomas and William, must have decided to support another claimant for the throne. Thomas had suffered at the time of Hastings' death and must have realised that he had had a lucky escape. Richard had obviously seen him as a lesser conspirator otherwise he too would have lost his head. His wife, Margaret Beaufort, was the mother of a claimant to the throne; in fact that claim was through her, although she seems to have been more ambitious for her son than for herself. It is doubtful, under the circumstances, whether she could have gained much support for her own claim and so passed her support to her son. Her marriage to Thomas Stanley would appear to be a retrograde one in the sense that by it she became Lady Stanley as her husband was a Baron. She could have aspired to a nobler rank. The Stanleys, however, were a powerful family in the north-west of England, the two brothers holding estates in Lancashire and Cheshire as well as in North Wales. Perhaps it was this Welsh connection that gave her the incentive to marry into the family. With her son's own Welsh ancestry he could claim support from both North and South Wales.

The other problem is that of "the Princes in the Tower." Although they disappeared from view during the summer of 1483 and have always been assumed to have died (been murdered) some time during August, any rising against Richard would have initially been to reinstate Edward V. Once it was believed that they were dead, would support have naturally gone to support a Lancastrian claimant? There were other Yorkist claimants around.

Richard successfully put down Buckingham's rebellion, which initially started in support of Edward V but later transferred its support to Henry. Was Richard always going to be threatened by Henry? It appears that once the princes were believed to be dead then the role of Margaret Beaufort became crucial in winning support for her son. After Buckingham's rebellion her estates were put under the control of her husband, who had supported Richard, as had his brother William, and their rewards were commensurate. The greater problem for Richard lay in the deaths firstly of his son and then of his wife. It was probably these events that gave the waverers the conviction that Richard was an unlucky king and that God had deserted him. He was only in his early thirties and could have married again and had more children; he could have lived to a good old age, for any heir thus produced to have attained manhood by the time he inherited the throne. Again, those forces which opposed him took advantage of the times and the situation to push the claims of Henry, and the chief mover in this must have been Henry's mother. Therefore Lady Margaret Beaufort must have played a crucial part in the decision of the Stanley brothers to support Henry.

The reasons why Sir William and Sir Thomas Stanley decided to support Henry Tudor, Earl of Richmond, in his attempt to capture the throne are rather complex. Sir Thomas had had a long-running dispute with Richard III when he was Duke of Gloucester, over the Harrington inheritance. Also, at the time of Hastings' execution he was imprisoned by Richard, although only for a short time. Both factors would have made him favour treason. While it is easy to see why Sir Thomas favoured Richmond's side it is not so easy to account for Sir William's change of allegiance.

In Sir William's case this was a major leap, as he had supported the Yorkist cause from the Battle of Blore Heath twenty-six years earlier. He had played no part in the "usurpation" of Richard. He had not been in London. He was probably either in Cheshire or with Edward V at Ludlow, although he is not mentioned as being present in Edward's train to Northampton. In 1485 he may have felt that the Yorkist dynasty was coming to an end and he would, therefore, support Henry. This change of a lifetime for him had unforeseeable consequences, in so far as Henry was an unknown quantity, having spent most of his life either in Wales or in France. If Sir William decided to change his allegiance, would he then live to regret it?

While the Stanleys were in correspondence with Richmond prior to the summer of 1485, possibly as early as May 1485,[1] matters did not come to a head until invasion was imminent. One final incident which may have played a part in Sir William Stanley's decision was the death on 12 August of his stepson and ward the young Earl of Worcester. The Worcester title became extinct and Sir William and his wife lost control of his lands.[2]

On 9 June 1485 King Richard moved to Nottingham and it was shortly after arriving there that Sir Thomas requested permission to visit his estates in Lancashire. The Croyland Chronicle says that he was only permitted to go on condition that he sent his son Lord Strange in his stead. However, there is some evidence that Lord Strange did not travel to Nottingham immediately, as he is believed to have been in Lancashire as late as the first week in August,[3] by which time Henry Tudor had landed on the Pembrokeshire coast (7 August).

Richard received news of Tudor's landing on 11 August and it is suggested that Sir William Stanley, at Holt, would have received the news then or slightly earlier. Sir Thomas, who was at Lathom, probably heard the news a day later. While Tudor continued his march through Wales, gathering support on the way, Sir Thomas gathered his troops in Lancashire and set out for the rendezvous. On 15 August 1485 Sir William set out with his Cheshire and North Wales men from his base at Holt, travelling via Nantwich where he encamped for the night. Sir Thomas, meanwhile, had reached Lichfield, fifty miles away, which would have made it impossible for a meeting between the two that night. At about this time, in Nottingham, Lord Strange was interrogated and confessed to the treason of his uncle Sir William and his cousin Sir John Savage.

On Tuesday 16 August Richmond left Shrewsbury, moving north-eastwards to try to join up with the Stanleys at Stafford. Sir Thomas left Lichfield and moved to Atherstone. Sir William Stanley moved south from Nantwich and rested after fifteen miles. The next day Richmond moved to Stafford, while Sir William Stanley marched to Stone and in the evening rode the eight miles to Stafford and had a meeting with him. This could very well have been their first meeting. Sir Thomas is known to have been at Atherstone, which, it being a good distance from Stafford, meant that it is unlikely that he joined them at this meeting. On Thursday Richmond moved to Rugeley while Sir William, keeping his force apart from the Tudor's, travelled behind and to the north it. On Friday 19 August Richmond entered Lichfield where he was greeted enthusiastically in a reception stage-managed by Sir William Stanley. Sir William then left, much to Richmond's dismay. No-one knows quite where he went. It has been suggested that he went to Tamworth to meet up with Sir Thomas, but Thomas had already left there three days earlier on 16 August. On the afternoon of the 19th Henry left Lichfield and headed for Tamworth, where the castle surrendered to his army. Richmond himself, meanwhile, had been overtaken by darkness and had lost touch with his army; he wandered around until he found a village where he stayed the night, rejoining his force the next day.[4]

On Saturday 20 August King Richard led his troops from Nottingham towards Leicester. Richmond rejoined his army at Tamworth and moved towards Atherstone where Sir Thomas and Sir William Stanley were encamped. Richmond met the Stanleys at either Atherstone or at Merevale Abbey a mile west of the village. This meeting was apparently cordial but Tudor failed to get them to unite their forces with his. Richmond camped with his force at Atherstone. The next day being Sunday, and the King's army moving into an advantageous position near Sutton Cheney, Richmond moved over the River Anker at Witherley Bridge and camped for the night on Whitemoors. Lord Stanley was stationed on the high ground near Higham on the Hill, moving towards Dadlington Hill and the right of Richmond's troops. Sir William Stanley marched his force of about 3,000 men from Pinwall via Sheepy Magna to the vicinity of Hanging Hill about a mile to the north of Richard's force at Ambien Hill.

The players being now all on stage there was only one possible course of action to be taken.

The next day was Monday 22 August.

ONE OF the main problems connected with the Battle of Bosworth, or "Redemore" Field, is its exact location. Much has been written in the last ten years in endeavouring to site the battlefield.[5] It is not my intention to join this debate. I am concerned only with the conduct of the battle and Sir William Stanley's part in it.

At dawn on 22 August the final disposition of the forces was made. King Richard's force was drawn up on Ambien Hill facing south. To the south-west was Richmond's force drawn up on Whitemoors, and to the south was the joint Stanley force of Sir William and Thomas Lord Stanley. It seems, however, that the position of the Stanleys cannot be described with confidence. Both Stanleys appear to have approached the battle as though they were uncommitted. Their position, being both south of the King and to the east of Richmond, could be seen as being of aid or attack to either force, and might indicate that they were not committed to either side and would await events.

The first movement came from Richmond's side. He moved his troops from Whitemoors and came down towards the Sutton Cheney road. In going along this he would pass close to the Stanley position, which would give them the opportunity to join his army as one force. However Sir Thomas, despite his son being in Richard's hands, made no move to join Richmond. He sent a handful of cavalrymen instead of his whole force and withdrew the rest of his army to a nearby hill where he waited out the battle, not taking any further part in it. As this manoeuvre was taking place Sir William brought his battalion up behind Richmond. Richard could see these manoeuvres taking place, and noting that Sir Thomas had withdrawn swore vengeance on the Stanleys for their betrayal. Richard ordered the immediate execution of Lord Strange but was persuaded to wait until all three Stanleys were in his hands.

The vanguards of both forces met on the south-west slope of Ambien Hill on the edge of the marsh, and it was here that most of the fighting took place. While this encounter was taking place Richard determined to enter the fray, and looking for the position of Richmond, and sighting him in the midst of a small group of supporters at some distance from the rest of his army, he drew together a small force for a cavalry charge towards his enemy. The charge met the resistance with clanging ferocity but Richmond's supporters rallied while Richmond himself stood firm. It was at this point that Sir William Stanley decided to join the battle, coming to the aid of Henry Tudor. All sources speak of King Richard's bravery at the end, but he was overwhelmed. He fell and was attacked and mutilated by Welsh pikemen. These could have been from Sir William Stanley's army since some of his men would certainly have been Welsh.

Once Richard was dead the battle was over. It had lasted little more than two hours. There were many nobility dead. Others, including Lord Lovell, had fled.[6] Sir Thomas Stanley now stirred himself to ride in pursuit of those who fled.

Sir William was granted the honour of the spoils from the field of battle and much booty found its way into his coffers at Holt Castle.[7] Some of the spoils also found its way into the hands of Thomas Lord Stanley.[8] Among the spoils was the crown of England found either lying on the ground, in a thorn bush, or taken from the helmet of the king. It is believed to have been found by Sir Reginald Bray,[9] but traditionally placed on the head of Richmond by either Sir William or Sir Thomas Stanley.[10]

It is possible that Sir Thomas did not actually meet with Richmond until well after the battle, and therefore it would be Sir William who performed the crowning. Sir Thomas later swore an oath that he did not meet with Richmond (now Henry VII) until 24 August.[11]

NOTES

1   Gill, p.128.
2   Calendar of Inquistions Post Mortem, Henry VII, vol.1, p.10.
3   Hammond (4), p.218.
4   ames, pp.58-61.
5   Foss.
6   Bennett (1), pp.99-120.
7   Ibid., p.121; PRO E/154/2/5, Inventory, p.26. Only a broken collar of roses and suns was found in 1495.
8   A 17th century inventory of Knowsley Hall noted hangings taken from Richard III's tent at Bosworth. Jones (1), p.22.
9   Packham, p.31.
10   Bennett (1), p.121.
11   Ibid., p.186 n.12.

St. Winefride's Well

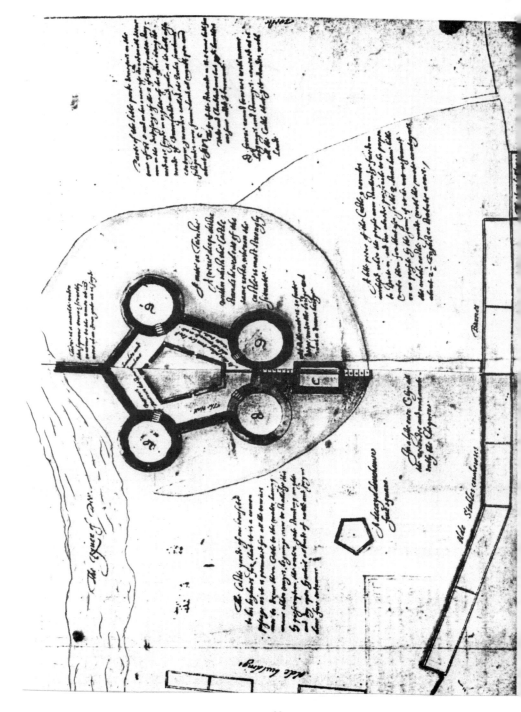

Chapter Five

Henry VII - Achievement

IMMEDIATELY after the Battle of Bosworth Henry Earl of Richmond, now Henry VII, began to imprint his own methods on the rule of England. However, two of the features of his reign were his fear of rebellion and his need for financial security. In order to maintain his authority he dated his reign from 21 August 1485, thus making all those who fought on Richard 's side traitors.[1]

Henry had lived most of his life in either Wales, France or Brittany and as a result was an unknown quantity in England. While he was unknown by his new subjects they in turn were unknown to him. His contact with them had been by emissary and letter and his fear of rebellion meant that he did not know whom among them he could trust.

Following the deaths of Edward Prince of Wales, at the Battle of Tewkesbury, and of Henry VI, Henry Tudor had become the chief Lancastrian claimant to the throne.

He remained in France for fifteen years after this, from 1471 to 1485, and during this period he relied on messages of encouragement from his mother and other supporters to sustain any ambitions to take the English throne for himself. It was not until the death of Edward IV and the disappearance of the princes in the Tower that he took an oath on Christmas day 1483 that he would marry Elizabeth of York on wresting the crown from Richard III. This led to more support from those, mainly southerners, disaffected to the Yorkists, and he finally landed near Milford Haven in August 1485. To the Welsh he was Llewelyn come again and they flocked to him, but this does not explain why the English nobility and Sir William Stanley and Lord Thomas took his part. Here it must have been the influence of Lady Stanley, Margaret Beaufort, the mother of Henry, which brought Lord Stanley to forsake the habit of a lifetime and commit himself to a definite course of action rather than managing to remain uncommitted until it was all over. Even so, this still does not explain why Sir William, who had supported the House of York all his life, should turn against his liege lord and support Henry at this crucial moment in time.

After Richard III's defeat at the Battle of Bosworth Henry became the *de facto* monarch and immediately set about consolidating his position.

He arranged matters so that his right to the throne would be unquestioned, in other words he claimed the kingship by birth, rather than by the gift of any individual or group or even through his marriage to Elizabeth of York. Consequently, while he issued writs for Parliament to meet on 7 November 1485, he arranged his coronation for eight days before this, on 31 October, when he was crowned with great ceremony in Westminster Abbey. The Archbishop of Canterbury was too feeble to perform more than the crowning and anointing and it was left to Bishop Morton of Ely and Bishop Courtenay of Exeter to conduct the rest of the ceremony. In the ceremonial the laymen closest to Henry were his uncle Jasper Tudor Earl of Pembroke and his step-father Lord Stanley[2] who had been created Earl of Derby in a ceremony in the Tower of London on 27 October.[3]

At the Parliament an Act was passed declaring that Henry's right to rule was by inheritance and not by conquest. Acts of Attainder were passed on his defeated enemies at Bosworth, and he was granted the revenue of the Customs for life. Titulus Regius, the petition in which Richard III had been asked by Parliament to take the crown, was repealed unread.[4] By doing so he withdrew the imputation of illegitimacy from the children of Edward IV. Parliament also urged Henry to fulfil his promise to marry the newly legitimized Elizabeth. A Papal dispensation was needed as they were fourth cousins twice removed, and the Papal bull, when it arrived, reinforced Henry's claim to the throne as it threatened to ex-communicate anyone who challenged his kingship.

The royal marriage was performed on 18 January 1486 at Westminster, but Henry and Elizabeth had perhaps already been living together and she was possibly pregnant with Prince Arthur when the ceremony took place. She had been promised a coronation when her child was born.[5]

Honours and rewards had been speedily granted to those who had supported Henry in his exile. His uncle Jasper Tudor, as well as being restored to the earldom of Pembroke, was also created Duke of Bedford.[6] He also restored the dukedom of Buckingham to the seven year old Edward Stafford in recognition of his father's support of the Tudor cause. Bishop Morton was rewarded by being made Archbishop of Canterbury and also Lord Chancellor. Lord Stanley, now Earl of Derby, served as Lord High Steward at the coronation.[7] Although this position was one he held under Edward IV it had been given to Thomas Howard, Earl of Surrey, during the reign of Richard III.[8] The new Earl and Countess of Derby (the latter under her old title, Countess of Richmond) petitioned Parliament on 19 November 1485 *"praying that certain possessions...may be settled upon her in lieu of jointure and dower."* The petitioners were answered *'Soit fait come il est desire.'* [9] Thus it would appear that Margaret Beaufort's estates were returned to her from her husband's keeping, to which they were transferred by Richard III after Buckingham's rebellion in 1483.

Where was Sir William Stanley in all this? It was, after all, his intervention at the Battle of Bosworth which had made victory for Henry certain. By early September 1485 he had already been made the king's Chamberlain, as on 17 September he was granted in tail male the manor of Hunnesdon in Hertfordshire in that office.[10] On 23 September he was made one of the Knights of Receipt of the Exchequer.[11]

On the first day of the Parliament, 7 November, Sir William petitioned the king in Parliament stating that

> *"he was seized of certain manors, castles etc ... of great value, and which he had of grant from Richard III in exchange for other manors etc, but which said grant he feared is not sure and sufficient in law. He therefore prays the king, in consideration of the true and faithful service of him the said William Stanley, that the king will ordain and enact that he the said William Stanley and his heirs shall possess, enjoy and inherit the said manors etc without let, impediment, interruption or impeachment, for ever etc."* The king answered, *'Soit fait come il est desire.'*[12]

On 24 January 1486 Sir William was made Constable of Caernarfon Castle and Captain of the town of Caernarfon,[13] and on 2 February Justice of North Wales.[14] On 25 February he was made one of the commissioners for Mines in England and Wales.[15] He also received many small grants, but nothing on the scale of the earldom given to his brother. However, as well as the appointment as Chamberlain to the king he was made a Knight of the Garter before 27 May 1487. His enrolment was to fill the place of Richard, 5th Duke of York.[16] This is ironic in that it was Perkin Warbeck's imposture of Richard Duke of York which was to lead to Sir William's death.

Of the appointments given to Sir William the most important politically was the position of king's Chamberlain or Chamberlain of the Household. Previous holders of the office under Edward IV and Richard III had been William Lord Hastings and Francis Viscount Lovell. The duties involved overseeing the *"Kinges chaumbres and the astate made therein to be according, first, for all the aray longing to his propyr royall person, for his propyr beddes, for his propyr boarde at mele tymez for the diligent doyng in servyng thereof, to his honour and pleasure etc."*[17] Although many of the duties could be assigned to deputies the role gave Sir William Stanley the oversight of the maintenance of the king's majesty, a significant rôle when appearance was very important.

In the spring of 1486 Henry went on a lengthy progress through the eastern counties, Lincolnshire and Yorkshire, to show himself in areas which had been predominantly Yorkist. Henry kept Easter in Lincoln and while there heard of a rebellion led by Lord Lovell and the Stafford brothers, Humphrey and Thomas. However, their army melted away when Henry declared that all rebels who laid down their arms would be pardoned. The leaders escaped, Lovell to friends in Flanders and the Staffords to sanctuary at Abingdon Abbey. Henry had them dragged from the Abbey and imprisoned in the Tower. Humphrey Stafford was later executed as an example, whilst Thomas submitted and remained loyal.[18]

Henry returned to London and before the summer ended went to Winchester where on 20 September 1486 Prince Arthur was born. With a male heir uniting York and Lancaster the Tudor line seemed assured.[19] Once again there was talk of the coronation of Queen Elizabeth but Henry demurred.

The winter of 1486 saw discontent which culminated in what has become known as the "Lambert Simnel rebellion." There is some doubt as to who Lambert Simnel really was,[20] but whoever he was he pretended firstly to be the presumed-dead Richard Duke of York, younger son of Edward IV, and then the Earl of Warwick, who was imprisoned in the Tower.[21] Among those who flocked to his cause was Francis Lord Lovell, the sometime stepson of Sir William Stanley.

It is one of history's mysteries that a pretender/impostor such as Simnel should have presented himself at this time, when there was a perfectly good candidate in John de la Pole, Earl of Lincoln, nephew of Richard III and Richard's chosen heir after the death of his son. Perhaps the conspirators put up an impostor in order to gauge the response and support for the Yorkist cause. If this was the idea it did not work, as Lincoln joined the support for Simnel rather than support coming across to him.[22]

None of the Stanleys became involved in the rebellion. Whether this was because they were content with the status quo, or because they had received rewards for past services, or recognised the futility of the enterprise, is not certain.

The first main event of the rebellion was the crowning of the impostor in the Cathedral of Christchurch, Dublin, on Ascension Day, 24 May 1487.[23] On 4 June Lincoln and the army landed at Furness in Lancashire, marched across the Pennines and turned south. Lincoln received less support than he had hoped and had to depend on German and Irish troops in the battle to come. The rebellion only lasted a short time, resulting in the Battle of Stoke (East Stoke, near Newark) on 16 June 1487, in which Henry's army defeated the rebels. On the field 4,000 rebels lay dead, including John de la Pole, Earl of Lincoln. Francis Lovell disappeared. Speculation suggested that he had drowned in the Trent, though the discovery in the early 18th century of a skeleton walled up at his old home at Minster Lovell seems to show that he perhaps managed to escape as far as Oxfordshire.[24]

Towards the end of June there were disturbances in Herefordshire around the town of Leominster, and the reports and submissions to the Court of Star Chamber implicate Sir Thomas Cornwall, Sir Richard Corbet and Sir Richard Croft. All three were Justices of the Peace for Herefordshire, with Sir Richard Corbet also being the stepson of Sir William Stanley. Sir Richard Croft was Treasurer of the King's Household and a trusted councillor of King Henry. Among the accusations levelled were that a servant of Sir Richard Croft had arrested two men who wore the livery of the Lord Chamberlain Sir William Stanley. A later submission said that Edward Croft, son of Sir Richard Croft, had openly called the Lord Chamberlain and Sir Richard Corbet traitors when their men, wearing the Lord Chamberlain's livery, were on their way to support the king at Stoke Field. There is no evidence of what subsequent action was taken, but a servant of Sir Richard Croft, Thomas Acton, was given a free pardon on 3 February 1488 for all offences committed before 20 August 1487. Perhaps this included his arresting those in the Lord Chamberlain's livery.[25] Whatever the nature of the treason alleged against Sir William Stanley, there is now no evidence to tell. The whole incident could be one of local nobles trying to increase their own power at the expense of others during a troubled period, or one royal household officer, Sir Richard Croft, trying to out-manoeuvre another - in this instance the Lord Chamberlain - or simply a reflection of the uncertainty of the times.

FOLLOWING the Battle of Stoke Simnel himself was captured, made to confess his imposture and put to work in the king's kitchens (where he would have come under the management of Sir William Stanley as Chamberlain).

Henry suspected that Elizabeth Woodville was enmeshed in the Yorkist rebellion that gathered round Simnel, and acted swiftly by giving out that she had forfeited her rights to her dower estates by having agreed to deliver herself and her daughters to Richard III. Her estates were given to her daughter Elizabeth of York. He persuaded her to enter Bermondsey Abbey, and granted her a pension. She died in Bermondsey in 1492 and was buried at Windsor beside the coffin of Edward IV.[26]

One of the main reasons behind the rebellion was that Henry had delayed holding a coronation for the queen. Whether this was because he wanted to show that he was king in his own right and did not owe his throne to the descent of his wife, or because of the expense, is open to question. The first point, however, had surely been settled by the terms of the Papal dispensation granted in January 1486. The second point could be answered by saying that the expense of rebellion or civil war was much greater than the cost of a coronation.

Henry dealt severely with the rebels, but the scale of the rebellion showed him that he could expect trouble if he did not keep to his word. Consequently the queen was belatedly crowned on 25 November 1487.[27]

As Constable of England Thomas Stanley rode before the queen in her coronation procession to Westminster. His rich robe was trimmed with sables, and his daughter-in-law Lady Strange, dressed in crimson velvet, was one of six baronesses who attended the queen.[28]

When his eldest son Prince Arthur was three years old, in 1489, Henry made him Prince of Wales. The king issued to his nobles, including Sir William Stanley, scarlet robes of grain trimmed with miniver fur.[29] Sir William's robe was still in the Great Wardrobe at Holt Castle in January 1495 when the inventory of the contents was made by the king's commissioners.[30] On 26 November 1489 the prince was brought from Ashehurst to Sheen, where he visited his father, and then each in his own barge went down the Thames to London for the celebrations.[31] Sir William

Stanley, as the king's Chamberlain, would have been in the train of the king.

Until the Battle of Stoke had been won, as Henry himself admitted, he was too preoccupied with the everyday tasks of outwitting active and potential rebels to turn to the difficult problems of reforming the Crown estates fallen into decay. Financial maladministration had been part of the Lancastrian heritage. The Yorkist kings had proved better at managing the economy. If he was haunted by those secret fears touching his subjects' personal loyalty to him he was hardly less troubled by the fear of insolvency. For all his carefulness and greed in exploiting the Crown's revenues, he found the expenses of government mounting so that apart from a reserve of plate and chested treasure, he left no more than £9,100 in cash to his son.[32]

Henry VII tried to maintain his finances by confiscations. The lands and property which he had taken from the "traitors" who had fought against him at Bosworth were kept in his hands. He created very few new nobles to replace those whom he had deprived. He had created only one new earl, his step-father Lord Stanley, who, already being possessed of large estates in the north, did not need additional lands to maintain his status. He also raised his uncle Jasper Tudor to the rank of Duke of Bedford. Already an earl, his needs would be few. One way of rewarding loyal subjects was to bestow the Order of the Garter, and this he did to thirty-seven of his subjects during his reign.[33] One of these was, of course, Sir William Stanley.

In other words, Henry rewarded the undoubted support that he received from Sir William in the cheapest way possible. Sir William, while being a power in Cheshire and the Welsh borders, had few lands with which to maintain the status of a man of rank. To have elevated him to the peerage would have involved handing over manors, lands and revenues commensurate with that status. It is to Sir William's credit that he amassed the fortune that he did from the sources of revenue at his disposal. How he achieved this is not certain.

As has been noted, one of Henry's main concerns throughout his reign was cash. One of the Crown's sources of income was grants from Parliament in the form of taxes and only voted to pay for an army in times of war. Both Edward IV and Richard III had experienced problems in raising money this way and had resorted to benevolences, or forced loans, in order to raise the money that Parliament would not vote. The other main source of income was from the Crown lands. Edward IV had endeavoured to improve the income from the Duchy of Lancaster, with the help of Lord Stanley in Lancashire, and this system was continued under Sir Reginald Bray the Chancellor of the Duchy. Henry, however, had also asked Parliament to pass an Act of Resumption, which allowed him to recover Crown lands which had been granted away since 1455. He also acquired the lands which had belonged to the Houses of York and Lancaster, including the earldoms of Richmond, March and Warwick as well as the Principality of Wales. His efficient management of the Crown lands meant that the annual income rose from £29,000 in 1485 to £42,000 in 1509.[34] Other revenue included Customs duties, feudal dues and the profits of justice. The latter included fees paid for the legal writ or summons to court, and fines levied on the guilty for their crimes, which could include treason. He appears to have exploited the system to his financial advantage. The £10,000 fine on the Earl of Northumberland for ravishing a royal ward seems to come under this heading. He also used attainder to enlarge his treasure. We shall see how this affected Sir William Stanley later.

Henry also maintained his household at the same level as instituted by Edward IV, and it was not until 1526, when Thomas Cromwell sought to improve the financial running of the royal household, that changes were made.[35]

These two main threads, the security of his throne, and his ability to pay for it, run through Henry VII's reign, and are largely responsible for the fate of Sir William Stanley.

NOTES

1   Markham, p.251.
2   Williams, N., pp.36-37.
3   Bagley, p.23.
4   Campbell, vol.1, pp.122-23.
5   Williams, N., p.37.
6   Rogers, p.37.
7   Williams, N., pp.40-43.
8   Myers (1), p.87.
9   Campbell, vol.1, pp.134-35.
10 Ibid., p.7. Tail male. The situation where by only a son or other male relative can inherit the rank, position or property real or personal. Thus the daughters cannot inherit these items. The classic example of this situation is at the core of *Pride and Prejudice* by Jane Austen.
11 CPR 1485-94, p.11.
12 Campbell, vol.1, pp.138-39.
13 Op.cit., p.258.
14 Op.cit., p.271.
15 CPR 1485-94, p.69.
16 Shaw, vol.1, no.232. In place of no.215 Richard Duke of York.
17 Myers (1), pp.104-06.
18 Rogers, pp.19-20.
19 Williams, N., pp. 53-54.
20 Bennett (3), pp.41-55.
21 Smith, G., pp.498-536.
22 Bennett (3), pp.41-55.
23 Op.cit., p.5.
24 Op.cit., pp.100-01.
25 Bayne and Dunham, pp.79-85.
26 Williams, N., p.60.
27 Rogers, p.23.
28 Bagley, p.24.
29 Campbell, vol.2, pp.497-98.
30 PRO E/154/2/5 p.8.
31 Harvey, p.150.
32 Williams, N., p.173. Is it a coincidence that this is almost the exact sum that was found in Sir William Stanley's castle at Holt in January 1495?
33 Rogers, p.37.
34 Op.cit., pp.63-64.
35 Myers (1), p.48.

Part of Christopher Saxton's 1577 map of Cheshire.
Holt is on the River Dee, on the Denbighshire/
Cheshire border, Ridley to the east on the River
Wever near Peckforton.

36

Chapter Six

Cheshire

THE GEOGRAPHICAL position of the county of Cheshire made it very important both militarily and politically during the Middle Ages. Chester, and the ports on the Dee estuary, were essential for the embarking of soldiers for campaigning in Ireland, and its Customs ports were a valuable source of revenue for the Crown. Earlier, the proximity of Wales made Chester an important base for the subjugation of that troublesome principality.

The men of Cheshire were also a valuable resource. The Cheshire archers had been the bodyguard of Richard II in the final years of his reign. In 1393 an abortive rising of Cheshire men gave Richard II the idea of recruiting an army of Cheshire retainers. He commissioned Sir John Stanley, among others, to recruit this force in 1397. This was the same Sir John Stanley who later married the Lathom heiress.[1] The men of Cheshire also seem to have played an important part in the rebellion of 1403.[2]

The county of Cheshire was originally an independent earldom and then later became a county palatine, and in both these forms it lay outside the central administration of the kingdom until the 1530s.[3] Therefore the main administrative mechanisms of the Exchequer and the Chancery were significant in their independence from central control until the later Tudor dynasty swept away the palatinate privileges.[4] The county sent no members to Parliament at Westminster and was exempt from paying taxes voted by it. The county was administered by officers who were responsible only to the Earl of Chester, who was either the king or his eldest son. It was, therefore, important to the king that those officials should be men who were loyal to him.

The most important Cheshire officials were the Justice, the Chamberlain, the Sheriff and the Escheator, and in all four offices there are examples of hereditary tenure at this period.

The most important official of the county was the Justice, as it was through the Justice that the king communicated his wishes. For example, when the king requested a *mise* or tax from the palatinate, the Justice always headed the commission appointed to negotiate the grant with the people of Cheshire.[5] Outside the County Court the Justice presided over Eyres which met annually in the Hundreds of Cheshire. In the period 1450-90 the Justice of Cheshire rarely attended the County Court or Eyres in person, and the everyday work of the office was undertaken by a deputy or even a deputy's deputy.

In February 1440 William de la Pole, Duke of Suffolk, was granted the office of Justice of Chester, Flint and North Wales for life. In March 1442 he was reappointed, but then in December 1443 Suffolk and Sir Thomas Stanley were appointed Justices in survivorship. Suffolk was murdered in May 1450 and Sir Thomas Stanley remained sole Justice until his death in 1459. On 20 May 1452, while Stanley was still Justice, John Talbot, Viscount Lisle, was granted the office of Justice of Chester and Flint to take effect on the death of Stanley. However, he was killed at the Battle of Castillon in Guienne in 1453, and when Stanley died on 20 February 1459 John Talbot, 2nd Earl of Shrewsbury, was appointed Justice by Henry VI. It was a post to which Thomas Stanley's son would reasonably have expected to have been appointed, and this can be seen as cause for the Stanleys to have opposed the king at the Battle of Blore Heath. However, Shrewsbury was killed at the Battle of Northampton on 10 July 1460, and Thomas, 2nd Lord Stanley, was appointed temporarily to the post. He was subsequently appointed Justice for life on 1 January 1462 and remained in office except for a short period in 1471 until his death in 1504.[6]

The Chamberlain of Chester was the leading administrative officer in the palatinate and in the later fifteenth century the post bore some resemblance to the offices of Chancellor of England and the Sheriff of a normal English county. The Chamberlain had custody of the Chester seal and was responsible for making out and sealing writs and charters. He was also the chief financial officer, accounting to the king or earl for the issues of Cheshire and Flintshire. The Chamberlain's work was conducted at the Exchequer in Chester Castle. The Chamberlain was also included in the commissions appointed to negotiate the mises. By this period the post of Chamberlain had developed into one of the main privileges offered by the king or prince. It was held by northern gentlemen of distinction. During the early part of the century the post took on the aspect of a sinecure, with a deputy doing an increasing amount of the work. Thus the salary of the Chamberlain was £20 per annum, in contrast to the Justice, who received £100 per annum, although the Chamberlain was in a position to acquire wardships and marriages and turn these to a profitable advantage.

The Lancastrian Sir Richard Tunstall was appointed Chamberlain on 21 February 1457 for life. Tunstall had received many honours from Henry VI and fought against the Yorkists at Wakefield and Towton, after which he was declared a traitor by Edward IV and forfeited his lands.

Sir William Stanley was appointed Chamberlain for life on 2 May 1461. The appointment included the offices of Constable of Flint Castle and Sheriff and Raglor of Flintshire[7] for life. The actual work of the Chamberlain was carried out by deputies. Sir Richard Tunstall had nominated William Horton and John Massey as his deputies, and while no records of appointment of deputies by Sir William Stanley have survived it is possible that these two remained in office during the period of Sir William's chamberlainship, which ended with his death in 1495.

Despite the fact that the salary of the Chamberlain was only £20 *per annum* it may be that the accumulation of wealth was possible. It was in 1465 and 1467 that Sir William Stanley and John Pilkington were granted the lease of the King's Pool in Chester.[8] This was the stretch of the River Dee above the weir, the fishing of which was reserved to the king and the Abbot of St Werburg's Abbey. Subletting his interest in the King's Pool would give Sir William much-needed revenue.

The duties of the Chamberlain included the collection of the Customs at the Cheshire ports. The Customs accounts for Chester are extant for the years 1467-68.[9] The main income was from a prise of wine, which had become established as a permanent Custom at Chester in the late 13th century. Although the prisage belonged to the earl at the beginning of its collection, when the king retained the earldom in 1301 the Chester Chamberlain always accounted for the prise of wine. Prisage was exacted on denizens at the rate of 1 tun on ships laden with between 10 and 20 tuns, and 2 tuns on ship's cargo of 20 tuns or more. The Chamberlain also accounted for the Customs on alien wine imports after 1303. The rate was 2s. per tun. The subsidy of tunnage was never accounted for by the Chamberlain.

Until the reign of Edward IV the Chamberlain accounted for the receipts of the prise and Custom on wine only, and he rendered a nil return on wool, woolfells and hides imported through Chester. From the financial year 1464-65 the Chamberlain accounted for the first time for a Custom on iron, which subsequently became a regular palatinate duty. The rate was 2s. the tun and never varied, being levied on denizens and aliens alike. This reflected the changing trade of the port, in that Anglo-Spanish trade in iron was developing, in which Chester played a key role.[10]

It was in his capacity of Chamberlain that Sir William Stanley was commissioned by Edward IV to leave Northumberland in February 1463 to return to Cheshire to arrest all those men who had failed to join the king's expedition to Scotland.[11]

The position of Sheriff of Cheshire differed considerably from that of sheriff of an ordinary English county. The Cheshire Sheriff's influence did not reach beyond the county boundaries and was mainly concerned with the proceedings of the Chester County Court, where he played an important role in the administration of the judicial system. He was responsible for the execution of original and judicial writs and the composition of juries. He had his own court, or Tourn, which met annually in the Hundreds. He was not concerned with the financial position of the county, but he did collect the fines and amercements arising from the County Court and Eyres and the rents from farms and leases. He had close dealings with both the local Exchequer and the County Court. As there was no parliamentary representation of Cheshire he was not involved in elections.

He was paid £20 per annum, as was the Chamberlain. Occasionally he was asked to undertake other duties which resembled those of sheriffs elsewhere. In 1463 and 1466 he was commanded to make an array of all the men in the county to assist the king against rebellion in England and Wales, and in 1481 was ordered to arrest all ships which attempted to discharge cargo other than in the port of Chester.

Upon the death of the previous holder of the office, Sir William Stanley was appointed Sheriff of the county for life on 26 February 1466. This was the third most important office of the county palatine. This was added to his post of Chamberlain. He held both posts until 1489. As Sir William Stanley also played a role in national as well as regional affairs it is possible that he considered both posts as sinecures, with deputies actually doing the work. However, as he had homes at both Ridley and Nantwich and he had strong family, as well as political, connections with the county and the north-west it is possible that he saw these offices as the foundation for his influence and of his power base.

Under-sheriffs have been traced who served with Sir William Stanley, with the names of both Sir John Savage and Hugh Grimsditch occurring in this connection. Sir John Savage had married Catharine, sister of Thomas 2nd Lord Stanley and Sir William, and this family connection would strengthen the hold on the administration of Cheshire. Hugh Grimsditch also had close connections with Sir William Stanley. Together with John Massey he had leased the Bailiwick of the Forests of Delamere and Mondrem to Sir William in 1473, and in 1484 Sir William, as Chamberlain, appointed Grimsditch to the position of Bailiff of Nantwich Hundred for life.

The office of Escheator was not considered as prestigious as the other offices and the fee was only £10 per annum. The Escheator's main task was to conduct Inquisitions Post Mortem into the lands which had been held by deceased tenants-in-chief in the palatinate and to transfer the lands to the heirs. If the heir was under age, he had to arrange for guardianship and enquire into proof of age, and he also dealt with dower arrangements. Occasionally he enquired into lands held by outlaws. He may have worked with the Sheriff, who would have organized the County Court juries and gathered the Inquisition juries.[12]

It is possible to see from the above that between them Sir Thomas and Sir William Stanley controlled the major functions of the administration of Cheshire. In fact, after Sir William Stanley was attacked by the men from Nantwich on 29 September 1470 the perpetrators were brought before his brother Thomas as Justice to be tried.

By the date of Sir William Stanley's taking up his appointment as Chamberlain in 1461 it would appear that he was in possession of Ridley in the manor of Bromfield and Yale.[13] He is reputed to have built himself *"the finest gentleman's house in all of Chestyrshire"* at Ridley, probably at the time of his marriage to Joan Lovell.[14] The Lovell lands included parts of Nantwich and it is known that Sir William also had a house there in 1469.[15]

Soon after taking up his position of Chamberlain of Chester Sir William Stanley began to attract the attention of the local gentry. On 27 October 1462 Piers Warburton, esquire, engaged to serve Sir William Stanley for one hundred marks from the fee of the grant of Bromfield and Yale. This relationship developed into one of friendship which lasted until death. It was sealed more completely in 1487 when Piers' son John married Sir William's daughter Joan. Piers was Seneschal of Halton Castle in Cheshire, and while holding this position had been correspondent of Eleanor, wife of Thomas Lord Stanley, later Earl of Derby.[16] Piers moved his family from Warburton to his new house at Arley in about 1469, the tithe barn of which still stands. This new house is believed to have been built in emulation of the new house that Sir William had built at Ridley.[17]

This connection with the Warburtons ties Sir William into the Cheshire gentry, as in 1495 after the execution of Sir William, John Warburton was made Sheriff of the county.[18]

The Stanleys had much to do with the Delamere Forest. In 1437 Sir John Stanley had been appointed a Surveyor and Rider of Delamere and in 1462 Thomas Lord Stanley was made Master Forester, in which he was succeeded by Sir William Stanley in 1489. The Stanleys of Lathom were also Keepers of Stotwick Park from 1468 until nearly the end of the fifteenth century.[19]

Edward IV's decision to make Sir William Stanley Chamberlain of Cheshire in 1461 was an important one both for himself and Sir William. Throughout his reign Sir William Stanley supported Edward IV, even when Lord Stanley his brother joined with the Earl of Warwick in 1470. Sir William brought Cheshire men to join Edward IV on his return from Burgundy in 1471 and he played a significant part in the Battle of Tewkesbury. He also suffered indignities at the hands of Nantwich men because of his support of Edward IV. Cheshire appears to have been strongly Lancastrian in sympathy and it could well be that in appointing Sir William Stanley to the positions of both Chamberlain and Sheriff, and Thomas Stanley to the post of Justice, the Yorkist kings were using them to control a potentially rebellious county. When Henry VII came to the throne they had proved their administrative worth, and although the political complexion had changed they also had changed, and he retained them in their positions.

NOTES

1   Gillespie, pp.1-39; Clayton, p.68.
2   McNiven, pp.1-29.
3   Thornton, p.40.
4   Wilson, p.1.
5   Clayton, pp.142-243. The mise was a special grant made to the king or to the Prince of Wales as Earl of Chester. This grant was normally made on the accession of the king and when the king's son was created Prince of Wales and Earl of Chester. However, there were occasions when special *mises* were requested by the Crown, and two of these were granted in 1463-65 and 1474-76: Clayton, pp.48-49

6   Ibid, pp.143-50.
7   The Raglor, or *rhaglaw*, was the lord's principal representative in the Commote, which was the Welsh equivalent of an English Hundred. The term later became synonymous with Bailiff or Constable. The Raglor held his land rent-free during the term of his office.
8   Ibid., pp.162-72.
9   Wilson, p.117.
10 Ibid., pp.4-5.
11 McKelvey, p.77
12 Clayton, pp.172-82. Escheators were officials appointed by the Crown to deal with the ownership of land which lapsed or reverted to the king or lord of the manor on the death of the owner, and oversaw the transfer to the legal heir.
13 Croston, p.225; Ormerod, vol.2, p.298.
14 Foster, p.23; Croston, p.226, Ormerod, vol.2, p.298.
15 Clayton, p.108; McKelvey, p.152.
16 Croston, pp.225-26.
17 Foster, p.28.
18 Croston, p.227.
19 Driver, p.88.

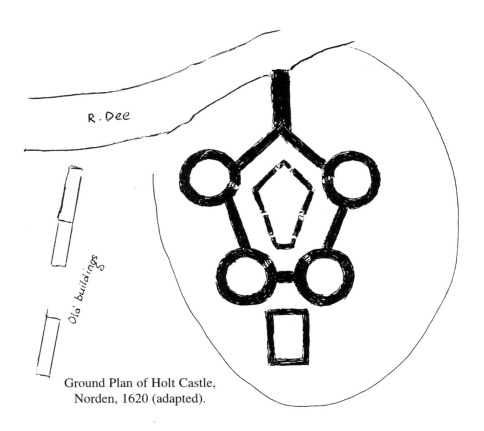

Ground Plan of Holt Castle,
Norden, 1620 (adapted).

Chapter Seven
Wales

THE PRINCIPALITY of Wales has from the Norman Conquest onwards been the site of dispute with the English kings. Once Chester was taken and became part of Norman England King William planted castles along the border with Wales to protect against invasion. With the completion of the conquest of Wales in 1283 arose the question of Marcher privilege. The Marcher lords had greater powers than their English counterparts, with privileges which they took by right and which were not granted to them by the king. In fact the king's writ did not run in the March, and the lords had their own courts and officers. A powerful lord could have his own sheriffs, chancery and chancellor with a great seal, and civil and criminal courts. He had rights to waifs and strays, treasure trove, goods of felons, wreck, wharfage and custom of strangers, among other privileges. In return for being allowed these freedoms the lord was expected to keep his castle safe from attack and be ready to serve the king when called upon to do so.[1]

By the Statute of Rhuddlan 1284, Wales was effectively divided into three parts: the south, based on Carmarthen; the north, based on Caernarfon; and the Welsh March.[2] The three northern shires of Anglesey, Caernarfon and Merioneth were under the Justice of Snowdon in Caernarfon; Cardigan and Carmarthen under the Justice of South Wales; Flint under the jurisdiction of Chester.[3]

In the reign of Henry IV at the beginning of the 15th century there was an attempt to ameliorate for the Welsh some of the effects of the Marcher privileges. In some respects the Welsh were effectively second class citizens, in that while they had their own laws and customs which were maintained, they were cut off from the government of their country by their English lords. No Englishman was to be convicted by a Welshman, an English burgess who married a Welshwoman was to lose his franchise and no Welshman was to hold office under the king or be of the council of any English lord.[4] Among those who had suffered under these laws was William ap William ap Griffith whose mother was Joan, daughter of Sir William Stanley of Hooton, who petitioned to be regarded as English. These laws were relaxed under Edward IV.[5]

The Stanley connection with Wales relates to their position within North Wales and the Marches.

Sir Thomas Stanley, the father of Sir William Stanley, was made Deputy-Justiciar of North Wales by William Duke of Suffolk, but resigned from the post in 1450 because he was "occupied in divers business whereby he has no leisure to exercise his office."[6] A relative, John Stanley, was Constable of Caernarfon Castle and Sheriff of Anglesey at the time of Richard Duke of York's return from

Ireland in 1449-50. Sir Thomas Stanley was instructed to find out all he could about the duke's arrival both in Cheshire and also, through his servants, in North Wales.[7] It would appear that by the time of Sir William Stanley's appointments in North Wales there was a tradition of Stanley involvement in the principality. The Stanleys had an extensive affinity within Wales which enabled them to work within the principality.[8]

Throughout his career Sir William Stanley was in a position of power along the Welsh border, and while most of his influence was in Cheshire, with which his family had strong historical ties, he also enjoyed a number of powerful appointments in North Wales. Some of these were complementary to his role in Cheshire, as at that time Flintshire still came under Cheshire administratively.

The main problem of Wales was that Welsh laws relating to marriage and land tenure were different from those of England. These were apparently administered by the English overlords, while the English settlers, who lived in the towns which grew up around the Edwardian castles, lived according to English law. It was not until 1543 in the reign of Henry VIII that English law was imposed upon the Welsh and Wales was united with England, ceasing to be a separate country.[9]

Approximately nine miles west of Sir William Stanley's house at Ridley, and just across the River Dee in what was a detached part of Flint, lies the village of Holt. A castle was built there between 1282 and 1311 and guarded a crossing of the Dee between Chester and Wrexham.[10] The castle was the scene in 1467 of a Great Court of the Lordships of Bromfield and Yale held before commissioners appointed by the Duke of Norfolk and Sir Edward Neville, Lord Abergavenny, to issue ordinances for the punishment of grave crimes committed within the lordship.[11]

The castle of Holt was built of red sandstone and at one time was quite extensive, being of a five-sided construction with a circular tower at each corner. A detached square tower, the exchequer, stood before the main land entrance. Built in a meadow beside the river, little now remains apart from the base of one of the towers, the result of being besieged during the Civil War. Given to the Grosvenor family, it was demolished between 1675 and 1683 when it provided building material for Sir Thomas Grosvenor's Eaton Hall.[12] Holt lies in the area of Bromfield and Yale (or Yal) and was first granted to Sir William Stanley on 10 December 1484 by Richard III as a reward for his support during Buckingham's rebellion the previous year; and it is this grant which gave Sir William Stanley the sobriquet by which he is known. But this was not the first grant that Sir William had received in Wales.

Since the area of Flintshire in North Wales was administered from Chester[13] it was logical that the Cheshire gentry would extend their influence to that area. Sir William had been granted "the lordship of Hope and Hopesdale, co. Flint" as early as 1 May 1461,[14] and it was confirmed on 16 July 1461.[15] The grant was at the supplication of the king's sister Anne, Duchess of Exeter[16] and made him in effect her trustee for those lands. The appointment also included the offices of Constable of Flint Castle and Sheriff and Raglor of Flintshire, for life.[17]

During the following years Sir William received several appointments and offices relating to the Welsh Marches, particularly in North Wales. On 29 September 1469 he was appointed Constable of Rhuddlan, Caernarfon and Beaumaris Castles for life,[18] and on 14 February 1470 he was appointed Steward of Denbigh for life.[19]

On 5 March 1475 he was granted the *"castle, lordship and manor of Chirke and Chirkeland in the marches of Wales...."* [20] This grant was in exchange for the lordship and manor of Skipton which was granted to the king's brother Richard Duke of Gloucester. While it meant that Sir William lost a very important position in the north, the transfer of his authority to Chirk ensured his power in the northern Welsh Marches and made him a Marcher lord.[21]

On 9 August 1478 Sir William was appointed to take muster *"at any suitable place near Conway of 300 men-at-arms and archers whom the king had ordered to Ireland."* [22]

In March 1483 he was included in a commission of Oyer and Terminer for the county of Hereford and the Welsh Marches.[23] With the change of king his position did not alter and on 12 November 1483 he was made Chief Justice of North Wales for life.[24] The payment for the post of King's Justice in North Wales was 100 marks per year.[25] On 17 September 1484, just before Sir William was granted Holt, the lordship of Hope and Hopesdale was granted to *"Thomas Stanley, knight, Lord Stanley, and George Stanley, knight, Lord le Strange, his son ... for their good service against the rebels."* [26]

Following Buckingham's rebellion in the autumn of 1483, on 10 December 1484 Richard III granted

> *"to William Stanley, knight of the body, and the heirs male of his body, for his good service against the rebels, of the castle, town, lordship and manor of Denasbrayn, the castle, town and lordship of Holt, the lordships, manors and lands called Hewlynton, Bromfeld, Yale, Wrexham, Almore, Burton, Hosseley, Ridley, Iscoyd, Hem, Cobham Almore, Cobham Iscoyd, Esclusham, Eglossecle, Ruyabon, Abunbury, Dymull, Morton, Bedwall, Pykhill, Sessewik, Sonford and Osseleston in the marches of Wales adjoining the county of Salop, and all castles, towns, lordships, manors, messuages, lands, rents, the rhaglawry of Merford and Hosseley ...."* [27]

AFTER THE accession of Henry VII Sir William was confirmed in the offices and lands which he had held under Richard III and was commissioned on 4 April 1486 (with others) to collect *"the myse in the counties of Chestre, Flint and North Wales"*[28] and his office of Justice for North Wales was also confirmed.[29]

On 24 January 1486 he was granted the wages and fees pertaining to the maintenance of the offices of Constable of Caernarfon Castle and Captain of the town, and the grant of a company of twenty-four soldiers at 4d a day for each soldier for the safe keeping of the said castle and town.[30] The payment for the post of Constable of Caernarfon Castle was £40 per year.[31] Sir William Stanley was also appointed, together with Jasper Tudor Duke of Bedford, the king's uncle, Thomas Earl of Derby, his brother, and others, to be a commissioner of the king's mines in England and Wales of tin, lead, copper, gold and silver.[32]

In July 1491, when King Henry was set to raise an army to invade France, Sir William was commissioned to muster, in Chester, the lordships of *"Bromfeld and Belt, Meryoneth, Caermartyn and Angelsea, Denbugh and Clome."*[33] In March 1493 he was appointed to the commission of the Marches to inquire into all offences, conspiracies and conventicles in the area of Salop, Hereford, Gloucester and Worcester and in all the Marches of Wales adjoining.[34]

In order to gain more control over the March, in about 1471 Edward IV established a Council in the Marches of Wales. This was to provide his son Edward Prince of Wales with a method of watching over the March. As the Prince was only a baby the real control was in the hands of his guardians, who were appointed by the king.[35] The Council usually met at Ludlow Castle or at Shrewsbury. The Council consisted of the Marcher Lords, clerics and the gentry of the border counties of both England and Wales. The first President of the Council of the Marches was Bishop John Alcock, who held the appointment from 1473 until 1501.[36] Thomas Lord Stanley, who was Justice of Chester at this time, acted as Vice-President of the Council and served as one of the judges. William Stanley as Chamberlain of Chester had to account to the Council for monies due to the prince,[37] as well as being a member of the Council by virtue of his lordships of Chirk and Bromfield and Yale.[38]

THROUGH THE offices and lands granted to Sir William Stanley he achieved the rank of Marcher lord and came, through his Constableships of the North Wales castles, to control access to Ireland and the defence of North Wales in case of attack. As Chief Justice of North Wales he would have been of the first importance in the principality, but this depended on his ability to control an unruly populace. All his Welsh possessions were forfeited on his attainder in 1495.

Holt became a place of special significance for Sir William. He used the keep as his strong-room, for it was here that his wealth in plate and jewels was found, and confiscated, by the king. His lands were not extensive and had been granted by the king, so his wealth must have come from his offices.

It was here also that during his time as lord of the manor of Holt the parish church of St Chad assumed its present appearance, and the present font was installed. The font is octagonal in structure and each face is emblazoned with heraldic devices which illustrate the history of Holt up to the late fifteenth century. The earliest representation is that of Warenne in Norman times, through to Henry VII. The devices include the boar of Richard III, which dates the font before 1495 when Sir William was executed as a traitor. No one following would have included this emblem. Sir William owed his lordship to Richard III.[39]

One other place in North Wales bears testimony to Sir William and that is St Winefride's Well at Holywell. The well-house was rebuilt during the later part of the fifteenth century and bears much Stanley heraldry. Until recently it had been thought that Thomas Stanley, now Earl of Derby, and his wife were instrumental in this work. But it has now been suggested that it was Sir William and his wife Elizabeth Hopton who had the work done.[40] The ceiling bosses include the figures of a man and woman now thought to be Sir William and Lady Stanley, the wolf's head (the badge of Sir William Stanley) and the hop and tun for Elizabeth Hopton.

These building works were carried out during the period 1485 to 1495 and could surely be seen as penances for the betrayal of his Yorkist king, Richard III.

The absence of a tomb for Sir William, and the final destruction of both Holt Castle and the house at Ridley, mean that the font at Holt Church and St Winefride's Well at Holywell provide us with the only lasting memorials of Sir William Stanley.

NOTES

1   Skeel, pp. 3-9.
2   R.A.Griffiths, "Wales and the Marches" in Chrimes (1), p.146.
3   Skeel, pp.9-10.
4   Ibid., p.13.
5   Evans, p.15.
6   Griffiths, in Chrimes (1) [as n.4].
7   Griffiths (2), p.271.
8   Jones (1), p.15.
9   Smith, J.B., p.170.
10   Taylor, p.334.
11   Skeel, p.14.
12   Taylor, p.334.
13   Griffiths in Chrimes (1), p.146.
14   CPR Edward IV 1461-67, p.7.
15   CPR Edward IV 1461-67, p.9.
16   CPR Edward IV 1461-67, p.7.
17   Clayton, p.167.
18   Ibid..
19   Ibid.; CPR Edward IV 1467-77, p.183.
20   CPR Edward IV, 1467-77, p.183.
21   Skeel, p.290.
22   CPR 1476-85, p.121.

23   Ibid., p.345.
24   Ibid., p.368.
25   Horrox and Hammond, vol.3, p.257.
26   CPR 1476-85, p.476.
27   Ibid., p.516.
28   Campbell, vol.1, pp.409-10.
29   Ibid., p.271.
30   Ibid., p.258.
31   Horrox and Hammond, vol.3, p.251.
32   CPR Henry VII 1485-94, vol.1, p.69.
33   Ibid., p.353.
34   Ibid., p.441.
35   Griffiths in Chrimes, p.160.
36   Skeel, p.287.
37   McKelvey, p.135.
38   Skeel, p.290.
39   Dorling, p.101.
40   Jones and Underwood, p.150.

St. Winefride's Well

Chapter Eight[1]

Wives and Children

AS A YOUNGER son Sir William Stanley had no inherited wealth. All his lands, rents and honours came from the king, and what the king granted the king could take away. Consequently, in order to gain security and prestige, he sought an advantageous marriage, preferably to an heiress as Sir John Stanley had done.

His first marriage was to Joan Beaumont, daughter of John, 1st Viscount Beaumont, and took place some time after 12 November 1465.[2] Joan was the widow of John Lord Lovell and the mother of the heir, Francis Lord Lovell, born in 1454. Thus Sir William Stanley became the stepfather to a very valuable twelve year old - although only briefly, for Joan died in August 1466. On his mother's death Francis became a ward of the Earl of Warwick and Sir William Stanley lost control of the Lovell lands.[3] The marriage was of short duration and it is unlikely that Joan bore him a child. The dates indicate that she could have died in childbirth; however there is no evidence to suggest that she did.

Sir William's second marriage was to Elizabeth Hopton, daughter of Thomas Hopton of Hopton, Shropshire,[4] and joint heiress of her uncle Sir William Lucy. Sir William Lucy's heirs were the representatives of his two sisters, Eleanor, who married Thomas Hopton, and Maud, who married William Vaux of Harrowden.[5] Elizabeth had been widowed twice before. Her first husband, Sir Roger Corbet of Morton Corbet, Shropshire, had died in 1467 leaving one son, Richard, in the care of his mother. Richard Corbet married the daughter of Walter Devereux, Lord Ferrers of Chartley,[6] who bore him a son, Robert. Richard died on 6 December 1492 when Robert his heir was "sixteen and more"[7] and when Elizabeth herself died on 22 June 1498[8] Robert petitioned Henry VII for control of her estates, and a licence of entry was granted on 10 December 1498.[9] Thus Sir William gained control of the considerable Corbet estates, with the exception of those belonging to Richard Corbet, until his death in 1495.

In September 1467 Elizabeth had married her second husband John Tiptoft, the "Butcher" Earl of Worcester (1427-70) as his third wife. He had no surviving children at that time, so Elizabeth's son Edward, born on 14 July 1469, became Earl of Worcester following his father's execution on Tower Hill on 18 October 1470.[10] After their marriage, which took place some time after 1470, Elizabeth and Sir William Stanley were jointly awarded guardianship of the infant Earl of Worcester and his lands.[11] This meant that, at last, Sir William had control of wealth independent of the king.[12] This continued until 12 August 1485 when Edward died aged sixteen and the title lapsed, the estates passing to his father's sisters.[13]   It could be argued that this event influenced Sir William Stanley's change of loyalties at the Battle of Bosworth ten days later.

Sir William Lucy had died on 10 July 1460, having been slain at the second Battle of Northampton. However it was not until 16 November 1482 that Sir William Stanley and his wife Elizabeth were allowed *"to enter freely into all possessions in England and Wales and the marches late of the said William Lucy, Eleanor and Walter which should descend to her."* [14]

There is a certain amount of controversy over who was the mother of Sir William Stanley's children. Elizabeth Hopton cannot have been much less than 14 when she married Roger Corbett in 1447, therefore she must have been born in about 1433. She gave birth to her eldest son Richard Corbet in 1448. In 1468 at the age of thirty-five she married John Tiptoft, Earl of Worcester, and therefore she was about thirty-eight when she married Sir William Stanley some time in 1471. Although this would make her old for childbearing it is not impossible that she was the mother of all Sir William Stanley's legitimate children.[15]

Richard III, on the death of Edward IV, had sought to secure the support of Sir William Stanley by granting him the lordship of Bromfield and Yale, which includes Holt and Ridley, in December 1484. Ridley in Cheshire was where Sir William Stanley built himself a new house, keeping Holt Castle as his stronghold. The house at Ridley was described by Leland in 1540 as *"the fairest gentlemans house in all Cheshire."* [16]   It was a substantial building, which was accidentally destroyed by fire in 1700 leaving only a magnificent stone and brick gateway, now with the Egerton arms above it.[17] (After Sir William's execution in 1495 the land and lordship of Ridley were granted to Ralph Egerton.[18])

After changing sides at the Battle of Bosworth on 22 August 1485, thus helping Henry VII to the Crown, Sir William Stanley was rewarded by being confirmed in his Welsh lands, as well as being made Chamberlain of the Household and Knight of the Garter.[19]   In fact, when he was executed on 16 February 1495, it was reported that he was the wealthiest man in England.[20]

The inventory of Holt Castle and Ridley, which was made by the king's commissioners Sir Edward Stanley, Sir Edward Pickering and Henry Wyatt on 27 January 1495, show that although Holt was a castle and not primarily a residence, the furnishings which were kept there were of a high quality. They included tapestries, bed hangings, feather beds, sheets, counterpanes, and a Wardrobe containing among other items the scarlet robe trimmed with miniver fur given to Sir William Stanley at the investiture of Prince Arthur as Prince of Wales. The chapel was furnished with altar cloths, priest's vestments and missals as well as candlesticks and communion plate. There was also everyday plate in the form of ewers and bowls. The Treasury contained the main treasure, £9,000 in coins as well as plate and jewels, also the garnishing of a Yorkist collar of roses and suns which was broken and obviously dated from the previous reigns. Among the plate were items with the arms of the Earl of Worcester, which must have been kept after the death of Sir William's stepson in 1485 and not passed to the next heirs.[21]

There was left at Ridley much less fine cloth and plate, adding to the impression that Holt was Sir William Stanley's strong-room. The items left behind at Holt and Ridley would be the items not needed at the other houses in which Sir William and Lady Stanley resided. They would take with them their most valuable possessions as they moved from house to house, so these objects, however fine, would be the second class items not in regular use. Therefore the luxury of the living accommodation must have been of a very high standard. At the end, all the finest portable items were bundled up and carted away to swell the king's treasury.[22]

AS WELL AS the two sons that she had borne to her first two husbands, Elizabeth Hopton bore Sir William Stanley three children: a son William, and two daughters, Joan and Catherine.[23]

William was born after 1471, and while not taking part in the Battle of Bosworth, he was old enough in March 1489 to succeed his father as Sheriff of Cheshire. This office had been granted to Sir William Stanley for life on 26 February 1466. He also succeeded his father as Chamberlain of Cheshire, an office which father and son held continuously from 1461 to 1491. The constableships of Flint and Rhuddlan Castles had been granted to Sir William Stanley on 19 November 1489 with the promise that his son would obtain them later, while on the same day William had been appointed Sheriff of Flint for life.[24]

None of these offices seem to have survived the attainder on Sir William Stanley.

William the son married Joan, the daughter and heiress of Geoffrey Massey of Tatton in Cheshire, who bore him a daughter, also called Joan, in 1493. After his father's execution William, having lost all his offices, was relegated to the status of a minor country gentleman.[25] He died in 1498, the same year as his mother. His widow Joan married twice more but she had no son, and on her death in 1511 the Tatton estates passed to William Stanley's daughter Joan.[26]

This daughter married twice, first at the age of eight to John Ashton of Ashton-super-Mersey in Cheshire, who died childless in 1513, secondly to Sir Randle Brereton of Malpas in Cheshire. In 1570 Joan died aged seventy-seven. Her eldest son Richard Brereton died childless and the inheritance passed to the second son, Geffrey, who married Alice, daughter of Piers Leycester of Nether Tabley, in 1551. They had two children, of whom the son, Richard, inherited the Tatton estates in 1565. Richard married Dorothy, daughter of Sir Richard Egerton of Ridley, and when he died childless on 18 December 1598, the direct line of descent from Sir William Stanley's son ended.[27]

Sir William Stanley's daughter Joan married Sir John Warburton, the son and heir of Piers Warburton of Arley in Cheshire in 1487.[28] As the Warburtons were a long-established Cheshire family this was an advantageous marriage for both parties. The marriage cemented a long-standing friendship between Sir William Stanley and Piers Warburton. Piers Warburton had taken service with Sir William Stanley in 1461[29] and by the time of the marriage had long been a friend, to the extent of building a new house at Arley in emulation of the house Sir William Stanley had built at Ridley.[30] Part of the marriage contract between John Warburton and Joan Stanley covenanted *"to settle Sutton Hall etc on William, son of the same Sir William, for the use of Joanna (Joan) for life."* [31] On her death it was to revert to the Warburton family. A letter is in existence from Sir William to Piers Warburton, unfortunately not dated, but written from his house at Ridley, referring to his inability to join Piers in hunting deer in his park as he is busy "with Olde Dyk." There has been some speculation as to who or what "Olde Dyk" was. Originally it was thought that it referred to Richard III[32] but a later suggestion is that it was some ditching work on his Ridley estates.[33] Would Sir William have given up the chance of a good hunt in favour of improving his estates if it could be safely left to his servants to do? Surely the inference is that it was work for the king, in this instance Richard III. Whichever way it was he obviously put duty before pleasure.

John Warburton succeeded his father in 1495 to the Warburton estates and also to the Seneschalship of Halton, an office he held for life. Also, Henry VII appointed him Sheriff of Cheshire. After being knighted in 1504 he was again appointed Sheriff and in 1506 this appointment was confirmed for life.[34]

John Warburton and Joan Stanley had many children, and the line of Warburtons of Arley descended without a break until 1813 when Sir Peter Warburton died without an heir and the estates passed to his sister Emma. Emma's daughter and heir married Rowland Egerton, who took the name Egerton Warburton, and this family continued at Arley until the death of John Warburton in 1915.[35] His daughter and heir Elizabeth married the Hon. Desmond Flower, 10th Viscount Ashbrook, in 1934. Their son Michael Flower is the present owner of Arley.[36] Thus the Flowers are direct descendants of Sir William Stanley through the female line. They can also claim descent from Thomas, 1st Earl of Derby, as Sir Peter Warburton (died 1776) married Elizabeth, eldest daughter of the 11th Earl of Derby.[37]

The only available information about Sir William Stanley's second daughter, Catherine, is that she married Thomas Cocat of Holt.[38] Thomas Cocat would be a gentleman. The name Calcott or Caledecot, pronounced Cawcott, relates to the nearby village of the same name in Cheshire. The name Calcott appears in the list of burgage owners in Holt in 1620.[39]

Sir William Stanley also had at least one illegitimate son, Thomas, who was involved in the Perkin Warbeck plot and was imprisoned by Henry VII. He spent fifteen years in the Tower of London before being released by Henry VIII in either 1509 or 1510. As he could take service with no-one in England he went abroad and took service with the last Yorkist claimant to the throne, Richard de la Pole. However, de la Pole did not trust him and thought him one of Henry's spies.[40] Whatever the truth of this, when Richard de la Pole died at Pavia in Italy in 1525 the connection of Sir William Stanley with the Yorkist cause was ended.

SIR WILLIAM Stanley married each of his wives when his political fortunes appeared secure. As a younger son his financial fortunes depended on either preferment from the king, or making a "good" marriage as his great-grandfather had done. Both his wives were the widows of landed men, and heiresses in their own right. They were also the mothers of heirs who were still minors, and as a result Sir William Stanley by being granted control of his stepsons also controlled their fortunes. His first marriage was unfortunately brief, but his second lasted until his death, and gave him resources independent of the king. Sir William Stanley built himself a gentleman's residence in his adopted county which was admired at the time and after his death. He made good marriages for his son and one of his daughters to the heirs of local Cheshire gentry, but as all his possessions were confiscated at his attainder, he was unable to leave anything to his children. The fact that his son died shortly after his own death, leaving a daughter, meant that he was unable to found a dynasty as John Stanley had done. He was not to know that.

NOTES

1   Parts of this chapter appeared in *The Ricardian*, vol.IX, no.116 (March 1992), pp.206-10.
2   Sutton and Hammond, pp.399-400.
3   Ibid., p.368; DNB, Sir Francis Lovell.
4   DNB, Sir William Stanley.
5   Cokayne, Sir William Lucy.
6   Sutton and Hammond, p.236.
7   CIPM Henry VII, vol.1, p.476, no.117.
8   Ibid., vol.2, p.91, no.130.
9   Ibid., vol.2, part 3, p.175.
10 Sutton and Hammond, p.400.
11 Cokayne, vol.12, p.845, John Tiptoft, Earl of Worcester.
12 This is confirmed by the find of plate etc. bearing the Worcester arms at Holt in 1495. Jones (1), p.7, n.21; PRO E154/2/5 46406 p.17.
13 DNB John Tiptoft, Earl of Worcester.
14 CPR 1476-85, p.332.
15 My calculations (see Bibliography, Gidman). *The Complete Peerage* gives her age as 34 in 1461, which would make her nearly past childbearing age when she married SirWilliam. He could have married between Joan Lovell and Elizabeth Hopton but as yet no record has come to light.

16 Foster, p.24; Driver, p.85.

17 The date of the gateway is in doubt, as Pevsner and Hubbard in *The Buildings of England: Cheshire* (1971), p.319, thought it could be Elizabethan. Ormerod, vol.2, p.301, refers to it as being "Sir William Stanley's fabric."

18 Ormerod, vol.2, p298.

19 DNB, Sir William Stanley.

20 The fall of Sir William Stanley is believed to have increased the royal revenues by £1,000 a year: Elton, p.48. He is also reputed to have left 40,000 marks in cash, plate and jewels: Sutton and Hammond, p.399.

21 PRO E154/2/5 46406, p.17.

22 Ibid., pp.22-25.

23 DNB, Sir William Stanley.

24 Driver, p.118.

25 Jones (1), p.20, n.88.

26 Ormerod, vol.1, p.442; CPR Henry VII, vol.2, pt.1, p.42. William Stanley's widow Joan's second husband was Sir Edward Pickering, who had been appointed to the commission to look into Sir William Stanley's lands and who was appointed Chief and Master Steward of the manors or lordships of Holt, Bromfield and Yale and also Constable of the Castle of Holt untul his death in 1502.

27 Ormerod, vol.1, p.443. It is worth noting that although not the heiress, Dorothy was a descendant of the Egertons who acquired Sir William Stanley's former estates at Ridley.

28 Ormerod, vol.1, p.572.

29 Croston, p.225.

30 Foster, p.24.

31 Croston, p.227; Ormerod, vol.1, p.572.

32 DNB, Sir William Stanley.

33 Jones (2), p.236.

34 Croston, p.227.

35 Ormerod, vol.1, p.575.

36 Foster, p.32.

37 Ormerod, vol.1, p.575; Bagley, p.132.

38 DBN, Sir William Stanley.

39 Palmer, p.411.

40 Arthurson (2), p.405.

Gateway of Ridley, Sir William Stanley's main residence. The house was burnt down in 1700. The arms above the gate are those of the Egertons.

Chapter Nine
Trial and Execution

AT ABOUT the same time that Henry VII was having to contend with the rebellion which surrounded Lambert Simnel and which ended with the Battle of Stoke, he moved to contain any rebellion within his own household. At Henry's second Parliament, which ran from November to December 1487,[1] an Act was passed which empanelled a jury of members of the royal household to enquire into whether any household man below the rank of peer had conspired to murder the king or any councillor or the Steward, Treasurer or Controller of the Household. This Act also made such a conspiracy a felony.[2] This Act, showing that Henry was far from feeling safe even among his own household, would ultimately lead to the death of Sir William Stanley. It also led to the development of the Privy Chamber.

However, early in 1488 the prospects of Sir William Stanley were still looking good. On 4 February 1488 "Sir William Stanley, knight, the king's Chamberlain" was granted

> *"the manor or lordship of Longendendale, co. Chester, with the town of Tyngetewysyll [Tintwhistle?], the advowson of the church of Mottrum, the sixth part of the barony of Nantwich, the advowson of the chapel of St Nicholas there, the advowson of the third part of the other chapel of St Laurence there, another sixth part of the said barony sometime of William Brounyng: the third part of the manor of Monkescopenhall, and all the lands forfeited by Francis Lovell, Lord Lovell, in the town of Tyngeteswesyll, Nantwich and Monkecopenhale, or elsewhere in the County of Chester, under an act of the parliament held 7 November 1 Henry VII, to hold from Christmas 1 Henry VII."* [3]

This grant of Francis Lovell's lands pre-dates Lovell's disappearance after the Battle of Stoke and must relate to those lands forfeited after the Battle of Bosworth. In this way Sir William Stanley regained some lands which he had held through his marriage to Joan Lovell and which he lost on her death.

In 1489 there was a rising in the north of England centred on Yorkshire. This was in addition to the support such unrest had received from the north at the time of Buckingham's rebellion in 1486 and the Lambert Simnel rising in 1487. Each time the rising had been quashed and the rebels had been bound by bonds of loyalty not to rebel again. Yorkshire was a particular source of concern for Henry as the memory of Richard III's good government of the region could not lightly be forgotten.

It seems to have been part of Henry's strategy to grant unprofitable or unpopular offices to former rebels in order to contain rebellion in this region. In this way he could ask them, then force them, to carry out unpopular orders, thus dividing the potential leaders of rebellion from their followers; a technique he subsequently used to contain the ambition of an "overmighty" nobility. One example of this is the case of the Stanley family in Lancashire, with Henry granting the Earl of Derby and his sons the major offices in the Duchy and Palatinate of Lancaster and then obliging them to carry out unpopular measures such as collecting lapsed taxes from among their own tenants and servants.

Whether or not it was part of this strategy, Henry ordered Henry Percy, 4th Earl of Northumberland, to meet with tax protesters from Ayton in Cleveland at Thirsk in April 1489. Yorkshire's tax burden was already heavy and also the collection of previous taxes had been delayed. The population had been exempt from many taxes when Richard was Duke of Gloucester and could speak to the king on their behalf, as the agriculture was poor. If the protesters thought that Northumberland would support their pleas for relief they were to be disappointed, as Northumberland insisted that the taxes must be paid. He was then deserted by his retainers and murdered on 28 April. The rising culminated in the rebels entering York on 15 May. Meanwhile Henry gathered an army and moved towards York, and the rebels fled from York on 17 May[4]

The army Henry gathered took time to assemble as he was in Hertford and moved from there to Dunstable on 12 May with, among others, the Earl of Derby in his train. As the army moved slowly north more support was collected. On 16 May the Lord Chamberlain, Sir William Stanley, joined it at Leicester. On the same day a muster was made of Lancashire men who had come with Lord Strange. The army finally reached York on 22 May. But before this the rebels had surrendered and executions had begun taking place at Pontefract.[5]

Whether this rebellion was more substantial than a tax payers' dispute it is difficult to say. It had no men of quality at its head, it was not attempting to replace the king with a Yorkist claimant or a pretender, but was a demonstration of the populace against unpopular taxation which had been alleviated by the previous rÈgime. It gave Henry the knowledge that his throne was still not secure. If he could not collect his taxes he could not control the country. He was not king.

Perhaps the events of 1489 concentrated the mind of Henry on how he should proceed in relation to the nobility, for he had developed the idea of the Privy or Secret Chamber.[6] This method of controlling his Household did not come into full being until after 1495, but the groundwork was laid in the previous years.

In 1490 Sir William Stanley was still in favour. He was appointed to the council of Arthur as Prince of Wales and Earl of Chester, and signed as witness to the document of creation.[7]

THE IMMEDIATE cause of Sir William Stanley's death was the emergence of Perkin Warbeck.

In 1491 Perkin Warbeck, who is now generally considered to be an impostor, made his appearance on the Continent claiming to be Richard Duke of York, the younger son of Edward IV who had disappeared at the time of the accession of Richard III. He was received by Richard III's sister Margaret at the Court of Burgundy, and at the Court of Charles VIII in Paris.

Henry sent spies, among them Robert Clifford who, according to evidence later presented, had joined with the Steward of the King's Household, John Ratcliffe Lord Fitzwater, as early as 12 January 1493 to conspire to support the pretender. It was agreed that Clifford would act as go-between and offer the support of the conspirators to Margaret of Burgundy. On 10 February Sir Gilbert Debenham and Sir Humphrey Savage also joined the conspiracy.[8] Savage was the nephew of Sir William Stanley, being the son of his sister Catharine who had married Sir John Savage.[9] Whether or not it was through this family connection, Clifford finally managed to involve Sir William Stanley in the plot on 14 March 1493. Sir William is reported to have agreed to promise to assist Perkin Warbeck with all his resources on receipt of a signal,[10] and that if the claimant was who he said he was then he would not oppose him.[11] Clifford left for Burgundy. However, throughout 1493 and 1494 rumours of invasion and insurrection abounded, together with arrests and executions, but it was not until the autumn of 1494 that Clifford made his way back to England and to the pardon his friends had purchased from the king. He was said to have brought back with him the proofs of the conspirators' treachery.[12]

It may be that Clifford was acting disinterestedly in naming Sir William Stanley as one of the conspirators. But it is possible that he had personal motives for eliminating Stanley. In 1461, following the Battle of Towton, Sir William Stanley had been granted the manor and lordship of Skipton which had belonged to the Clifford family, and would thus have incurred the wrath of a Clifford who was now finally able to get his revenge.[13]

In the New Year of 1495 Henry took up residence in the Tower of London, bringing with him in his train many of the conspirators including those named by Clifford. While it is possible that the king, who had already been told of Sir William Stanley's complicity in the plot, needed Clifford's testimony before the Council in order to secure his execution, it is also possible that the king was only too ready to believe that his Chamberlain was guilty because he wanted him to be guilty. By losing both his Chamberlain and the Steward of his Household at the same time he could replace them with nonentities and retire behind the closed door of the Privy Chamber.[14]

With Sir William Stanley imprisoned in his quarters in the Tower the king moved to ascertain his value. On 27 January he appointed commissioners to look into his belongings at Holt Castle and at Ridley.[15] On 8 February he appointed a commission under Arthur, Prince of Wales (now nine years old), *"to enquire of the lands and possessions in North Wales and the marches thereof, and the counties of Chester, Flint and Salop of William Stanley, knight, attainted of high treason, and to take charge of same."*[16]

An attainder was an Act of Parliament which involved *"the loss of all the attainted's goods and the perpetual disinheritance of his heirs, so that they may be admitted neither to the paternal nor the maternal inheritance."*[17]

Before the trial proper there was an inquiry held on 3 February 1495 before Sir William Hussey, Chief Justice of the King's Bench, Sir Thomas Brian, Chief Justice of the Court of Common Pleas, William Danvers, Thomas Tremayne and John Vavasour.[18]

Sir William's trial took place in Westminster Hall on 6 and 7 February 1495, before the Duke of Buckingham, the Marquess of Dorset, the Earl of Arundel, Simon Digby and the Chief Justice of the King's Bench.[19] The only evidence against him was that he had said that if Perkin Warbeck was truly Richard Duke of York then he would not oppose him.[20] He was also charged with conspiring with Clifford to send support to Warbeck when he received Clifford's signal.[21] In response to the charge of treason he pleaded Not Guilty.[22]

If the charges were based only on what was said in the conversation which took place on 14 March 1493 with Sir Robert Clifford, then the evidence is very flimsy. However, it could be construed to contravene the Act of 1487 which made such a statement a felony. Thus Sir William was found guilty and sentenced to death. His execution was held on Tower Hill on 16 February at nine o'clock in the morning, where he was beheaded on the scaffold there.[23] Of the other conspirators who were arrested, Humphrey Savage was kept in prison and Lord Fitzwater was imprisoned in Guisnes Castle, from where he attempted to escape in November 1496. After this he was executed on 24 November 1496.[24] Sir William Stanley's bastard son Thomas was also caught up in the conspiracy, was captured and spent the next fifteen years in prison until released by Henry VIII in 1510.[25]

There has always been a strong feeling that William's death had been sought by the king because he wanted his cash. Stanley had amassed an immense fortune in plate and money at his castle of Holt, near Wrexham, until he was reported to be the wealthiest man in England. The inventories of Holt and Ridley show the extent of this fortune in furnishings, plate, jewels and coin. The cash alone comes to about £9,000, a sum almost equal to the amount that Henry bequeathed to his son Henry VIII.

Another theory is that William was becoming too ambitious, in that he wanted to be ennobled as his brother had been, and aspired to the title Earl of Chester, one traditionally granted to the eldest son of the king. Henry VII's eldest son Prince Arthur had been created Earl of Chester on 29 November 1490. As Sir

William was one of his Council, it would appear that this ambition, if it ever existed, was not realistic but more a pious hope. Even if the ambition had been voiced surely it would not have been enough to compass his death.

If Henry wanted Sir William's wealth then he had to find some way of getting rid of him, and the enlisting of Clifford to help in this would be a good move, as Clifford had resented William's being granted Skipton in Craven way back in 1464. But why have him reported as saying that if Perkin Warbeck was Richard of York he would not oppose him, if it was widely known that Richard Duke of York was dead? And while it was a treasonable remark it was also foolish, and Sir William had not survived the Wars of the Roses by making foolish remarks. Thus it would appear that any justification for his execution had to have been fabricated. Sir William was the king's uncle by marriage, a valued supporter and the man who was instrumental in putting Henry on the throne. Henry surely had nothing to fear from him, and so it is logical to assume that Henry was indeed after his wealth and used Clifford as *agent provocateur.*

Following Sir William's execution his body lay in St Peter ad Vincula in the Tower before being taken to the Convent at Syon for burial on 27 February at the king's expense. As the king had taken all his lands and impoverished his family it was left to him to bury him as an "act of mercy." The cost of the funeral appears in the king's expenses as £15.9s[27] Also the king paid £10 on the day of execution and later a further £31.0s.1d to pay the outstanding wages of Sir William's servants[28] While it was possible for the heirs of those attainted to have the Act of Attainder reversed by Henry VII, it usually cost the heir a great deal of money and took time. Sir William Stanley's heir, William Stanley, did not live long enough to have his father's attainder reversed even if it had been possible under the circumstances, and even if he could have afforded to purchase the estates his father had once held.[29]

There is of course another theory and that is that Perkin Warbeck was truly Richard Duke of York, who had not been killed on the orders of Richard III but was alive and well in 1494. If this was so then Henry had to find some way of discouraging support for Warbeck, and what better way than to execute several possible supporters including the man who was known to have put him on the throne, his step-uncle, Sir William Stanley. Although not a blood uncle, he was a powerful and wealthy magnate whose fate the nobility would watch in alarm.

Because of the conspiracy relating to Perkin Warbeck Henry was deprived of both the Chamberlain and the Steward of his Household; this made it easy for Henry to move from the Yorkist Chamber form of government to his own Privy Chamber government. If Sir William Stanley and Lord Fitzwater had not been trapped by the conspiracy the start of Henry's Privy Chamber would have been delayed and his sense of insecurity would have grown.

For Ricardians William's fate is seen as retribution for his betrayal of Richard III at Bosworth. But William had also betrayed himself at Bosworth. Throughout his life, until the Battle of Bosworth, he had supported the Yorkist cause, while his brother Thomas remained uncommitted and thus reaped many benefits. With his death his lifelong support of the House of York was ended.

This is, however, not quite the end of the story. In July 1495, after the attempted landing by Warbeck at Deal, Henry made a progress through the north of England, calling upon his mother and her husband, Thomas Stanley Earl of Derby, at Lathom House. The house had been recently enlarged with the addition of an Eagle Tower. It is rumoured that during his viewing over the house Henry arrived at the top of the Eagle Tower, from whence a good view of the county could be seen. While up there he overheard the jester whisper to the earl, *"Tom, remember Will,"* whereupon Henry left the tower in great haste and refused to go up again.[30]

IT WOULD appear that the execution of Sir William Stanley was the result of both King Henry's greed and his insecurity. Despite his victory at Bosworth he never trusted those who served him.

NOTES

1   Chrimes (2), p.78.
2   Starkey, p.75.
3   CPR Henry VII, vol.1, p.263.
4   Cunningham, pp.65-69.
5   Bennett (2), p.56-58.
6   Starkey, p.76.
7   Campbell, vol.2, pp.541-42.
8   Arthurson (2), p.62.
9   Hampton, no.28.
10 Arthurson (1), pp.62-63.
11 Bennett (2), p.58.
12 Arthurson (1), p.84.
13 See above, p.8.
14 Starkey, p.76.
15 PRO E/154/2/5 46406.
16 CPR Henry VII, vol.2, p.29.
17 Lander (1), p.127.
18 Archbold; Mount, p.10.
19 Arthurson (1), p.86.
20 Kendall (1), p.383.
21 Arthurson (1), p.152.
22 Archbold; Mount, pp.10-11.

23 Information from the Tower of London. Archbold says he was hung, drawn and quartered at Tyburn, which casts some doubt on the reliability of the document.
24 Arthurson (1), p.152.
25 Arthurson (2), p.417.
26 PRO E154/2/5 46406.
27 Nicholas, pp.181-82.
28 Arthurson (1), p.86.
29 Lander (2), pp.136-39
30 Draper, p.40

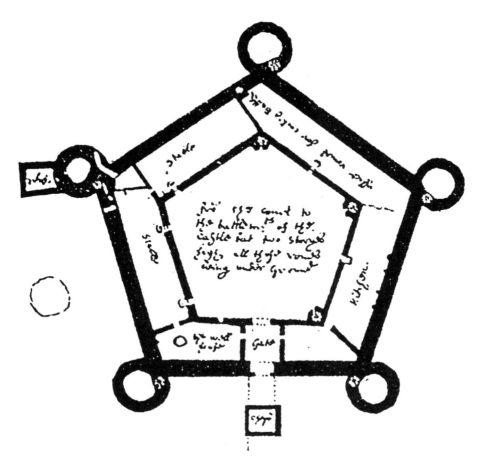

Ground Plan of Holt Castle, possibly 16th century (adapted from original).

Appendix 1
The Inventory of Holt and Ridley

THE INVENTORY of Sir William Stanley's house at Ridley was taken on 27 January 1495, and that of his Castle at Holt on 28 January. Two copies of each of the two inventories make up PRO (Public Record Office) manuscript **E/154/2/5**. The MS is bound and is in a good clear contemporary hand, not difficult to read. Each page is numbered consecutively in the top outer corner (right on right-hand pages, left on left-hand pages) in an early 19th century hand. Each leaf has also been numbered, in at least two sequences.

The MS starts at page 3, which is a fragment with a list of the king's commissioners in a hand different from the rest and harder to read. It appears to be their signatures. The inventory proper starts on page 5 as does this transcript. It is in six parts, as follows.

Inventory of Holt Castle	pages	5-19
Inventory of Ridley		20
[blank page]		21
Items to be removed *(to London?)*		22-25
Contents of Treasure House at Holt		26-27
[missing pages]		28-30
Inventory of Holt Castle *(copy)*		31-47
Inventory of Ridley *(copy)*		48-49

We here print only one copy of the inventory of Sir William's goods (pp.5-27), supplementing it from the other where the two texts differ. The list of the bags of coins in the Treasure House has been reduced to the number of bags and their total contents. Numbers have been left as roman numerals, as in the original. The spelling is as in the original, but punctuation has been added.

[INVENTORY OF SIR WILLIAM STANLEY GOODDS *(p.31)*]

[p.5] Memorandum that the xxviijth day of Janyver the xth yere of the Raigne of our Souveraigne lorde king Henry the vijth, Sir Edward Stanley knight for our said Souveraigne lordes body, Sir Edward Pekering knight and Henry Wiatt[1] [Esquier *(p.33)*] Commissioners to our said Souveraigne lorde by the Commaundement of our said Souveraigne lorde toke a veu of all the Castalles landes places and goodes belonging to Sir William Stanley late lorde Chamberlain aswell in the Castell of the Holte as in other places, in whiche Castell the said Commyssioners have founde thise parcells of Stuffe and goodes ensuyng.

The Chequer Toure

Furst in the said Toure in the upper Chambre a Federbed with a bolster of the Same, ij Sheetes of ij bredes, ij blankettes and ij Coverlettes.

Item under that is the entryng of the gate and nothing therin but a pair of Stokkes.

Item under the said Entre a Chambre and nothing therin.

The Secunde gate

Furst in the upper Chambre of the said gate ij beddes with ij mattres, ij bolsters of woll, ij pair of blankettes, ij pair of Shetes of ij bredes and iiij Coverlettes.

Item under that the Porters Logge wherin is a bedstede, a mattres, a bolster of woll, ij Sheetes of ij bredes, [ij blanketes *interlineated*] iiij² Coverlettes, a borde, ij Tristelles and ij fourmes. And betwixt the gattes ij great Serpentyns of Ireon and iiij Chambres.

[p.6] Item in a house under that a well with a Boket and a Chayne. In the Same house ij pipes of leede lawse, ij gutters covered with leede, a longe pipe of leede for the pumpe, and a pipe of leed that comys out of the Court.

Item uppon the Right hande in entryng the gatte a Toure Callid the Glasiers Toure In the upper Chambre a fedderbed with a bolster of the same, ij pillows, ij Sheetes of iij bredes, ij fustians, ij white Coverlettes and a Counterpoint of Tapestriwark lyned, a Sperver and Tester of grein Sarsenet with Curtens of the same.

Item the said Chambre hongen with iiij olde hinginges of Rede Saye and a Cupbord Clothe of the same, with a Cusshen of Tapestry Work.

Item uppon a paillet in the same Chambre a mattres, a bolster of woll, ij blankettes, ij Sheetes of ij Bredes and ij Coverlettes.

Item a Chambre under that and nothing therin

Item in a Chambre under that in the same Toure a fedderbed, a bolster of the same, ij Sheetes of hollande, oon of ij bredes and a nother of iij bredes, ij fustians, ij Coverlettes and a Conterpoint of Tapestry work with a Cusshen of the same, a Sperver with a Tester of grene velvet browdered with lyons of golde and Flourdelices of the same.

Item the said Chambre hongen with iij peces of [olde *(p.34)*] Tapestry work with a Cupbord Clothe of the same.

Item uppon a paillet in the same Chambre a mattres with a bolster of wolle, ij blankettes, ij Sheetes of ij bredes and ij Coverlettes [white *(p.34)*]

Item under the same Chambre a Dungeon and nothing therin.

Item next the said Toure on the same side a great Chambre with a bedsted therin and nothing els.

[p.7]

Item under that a house where thai make Candells in, wherin is a sirayn of woll.

Item under that is the wine Celler with a pipe and a halfe of Caparike.

Item next that the larder house wherin is a great saltyng Tubbe with viij Oxen therein by estimacion, ij bigge poudring Tubbis with ij bestes in the same, ij Soussing Tubbis, ij lytell Tubbis with venoyson in Salte, ij hogges heedys of vergeous and iij bakon flichis.

Item next that the kechin, wherin is ix hoole pannys great and Smale, iij olde pannys brokin, viij pottes of brasse of new Stuffe, viij olde brase pottes broken, a Brase potte Sett in a fournes, a nother potte Sette in the erthe, a brasen morter and a pestell of Iron, a litell posnet and a potte [of brase *(p.35)*] of my lades, vj Spittes great and Smale, iij friyng pannys great and Smale and a grater for brede.

Item ij Dousyn of newe peuter platers, iij dozen of olde platers, xij newe Disshis, xxvj olde Disshis, vij newe Sausers, xxviij olde Sausers, ij new Chargeours, v olde Chargeours, iij ladels of latton, ij Scomers, Dressing bordes and other bords vj, a pipe full of Salte and iij Tubbis with Salte, a payer of mustard quernys. And in the Cokes Chambre a Trowgh for Salte and a faire Table.

Item next the said kechin a Toure Callid the goldsmyths Toure. In the upper Chambre which is for Straungers, a Fedderbed and a bolster of the Same, ij blankettes, ij Sheetes of hollande oon of ij bredes and a nother of iij bredes, ij Coverlettes, a Conterpoint of grene verdures, a Ceeler and Tester of grene Saye with Curtens of the same, hongen with ij olde peeces of Reede Saye, with a Cupbord Clothe of the Same and an olde Cusshen.

[p.8] Item uppon a paillet in the said Chambre a mattres and a bolster of woll, ij blankentes *[sic]*, ij Sheetes of ij Bredes, and ij Coverlettes.

Item under that in the said Toure is the Conestables Chambre with a mattres and a bolster of woll, ij blankettes, ij Sheetes of ij bredes and ij Coverlettes.

Item under that in the said Toure a house for prisonners

Item betwixst that and the next Toure a Chambre for gentilwomen with a matttres and a bolster of woll, ij blankettes, ij Sheetes of ij bredes and ij Coverlettes.

Item under that a great Chambre with a bedstede and woode for my lady and nothing els.

Item next that my lades Chambre with a Federbed of Downe and a bolster of the Same, ij Fustians, ij Sheetes of iij bredes, ij Coverlettes and a quylte, a Celer and Tester of yellow Sarsenet with Curtens of Tawny sarsenet, and a Counterpoint of the same, hongen with iij peeces of olde Rede Saye and a Cupbord Clothe of the Same.

Item under that an house with Diverse olde Sadels and horsharnes, wherof ij Sadels is Covered with Crimosyn velvet and oon with Clothe of golde, and a sertayn of olde bridell bittes and olde horshoon.

Item next that a nother Toure wherof the upper Chambre is Callid the high wardrop, uppon a presse in the said wardrop is a good parlament Roobe of Scarlet furred with mynever and a hode [p.9] to the same, an olde Roobe and a gowne of Scarlet unfurrid and a hoode to the same, a quarter of a gowne of Scarlet and iij sleves, ij olde gownes of Sangwyn velvet oon wantyng a sleve, ij quarters of a gowne of olde Sangwyn velvet uppon velvet, a mantell with a Trayn of velvet of the same Coulour for a gentylwoman, an olde gowne of velvet of the same Coulour for a gentylwoman, iiij quarters of a gowne of velvet for a man of the same Coulour, ij Mantells of Saint George of blewe velvet lyned with [white (p.37)] Sarsenet, a white gowne Single whiche hadde garters uppon it, a shorte gowne of Crimosyn Clothe unlyned, ij Doublettes of blake Satyn of the Which oon was geven to the Steward, an olde Doublet of Crimosyn Satyn whiche was geven to William Damport, a Single gowne of murrey Clothe with garters, a demy gowne of blake Clothe unlyned, a Journet of goldsmyths warke, ij olde Cape de hustys oon lyned with velvet and a nother with Satyn, an olde Jaket of velvet unlyned, an olde Jaket of Russet, a Jaket of white Clothe with a Rede Crose and a butterfly ther uppon, a Shorte gowne of grene with holys, a nother Shorte gowne of Murrey with holys, an olde petycote of Scarlet, iiij Shredes of blak Clothe of the Shortyng of a gowne, iij quarters and ij Sleves of a Jaket of Scarlet, ij Remanentes of kendall oon of kentysh kendall and the other of blake kendall, ij quarters of a Journet of velvet, a Side Cremosyn gowne lyned with blak velvet, a longe violet gowne lyned with Tawne velvet, a Demy blake Chamelet gowne lyned with blak frees, an olde White gowne unlyned, iij bonettes and a Russet hatte.

Item uppon a nother presse in the said Wardrop a good bedde of bawdekyn [with S *deleted*] Browdred with Swannes of [3] [p.10] golde and a Conterpoint of the Same wantyng a Swanne, with iij Curtens of Rede sarsenet.

Item a good Sperver of Clothe of golde with a Tester of the same and Curtens of blewe Sarsenet.

Item a good Sperver of Crimosyn velvet with Curtens of sarsenet horsfleshe Coulour.

Item a good Sperver of panys of blew velvet and white Damaske with Curtens of grene Sarsenet.

Item a good Sperver of Clothe of golde with Curtens of Tawney Sarsenet. [Item a good bed of bawdekyn *inserted in another hand.*]

Item an olde Ceeler and Tester of Tawney velvet browdred with lyons of golde and bordured with flourdelices of golde.

Item a Travers of grene sarsenet, an olde Curten of Tawney sarsenet and an olde Curten of blake sarsenet. Item v Cusshens of grene velvet metly good, ij good Cusshens of Rede velvet barrid with clothe of golde, iij olde Cusshens of bawdekyn, a good Cusshen of Russet Clothe of golde and a good Cusshen of blewe bawdekyn.

Item in a Coffre in the said wardrop xvj pair of Sheetes and a Sheete[4] of iij bredes which be good.

Item uppon a nother presse in the said wardrop x good peeces of verdures bordured with olde Tentes, Contayning every of thaim in length iiij yardes scante and in depnes every of thaim iij yardes half.

Item iij good peces of Conterfait Aras of the Story of Olyfarnus, ij of thaim Contayning in lengthe ether of thaim viij yardes and a half and the iij[de] xj yardes, and every of thaym in depnes iij yardes half.

Item a litell pece of verdure Contayning in length a yarde scante and in depnes iij yardes half.

[p.11] Item iij good peces of verdurs with Connys, oon of thaim contayning in lengthe viij yardes and ij peces every of thaim in lengthe vj yardes, and in depnes every of thaim iiij yardes.

Item iiij good peces of pale verdurs, oon of thaim Contayning in lengthe iiij yardes and iij every of thaim iij yardes half of lengthe, and contaynes every of thaim in depnes iij yardes half.

Item uppon a nother presse in the said wardrop viij good peces of Conterfait Aras of the Seege of Jerusalem, oon peece Contayning in length xij yardes, a nother pece viij yardes half, a nother pece vij yardes, a nother pece vj yardes scant, a nother iiij yardes, a nother iij yardes quarter, a nother iiij yardes, and a nother iij yardes quarter. And every of thaim Contayneth in depnes iiij yardes.

Item vij good peeces of Conterfait Arras of huntyng and wilde bestes, v of thaim Contayning in lengthe every pece vj yardys scante, and ij of thaim Contayneth in length every pece iiij yardes, and every of thaim Contaynes in depnes iiij yardes.

Item a faire Conterpoint of Conterfait Aras of Ester and After.

Item a faire Conterpoint of Smale verdures with Birdys and Connys.

Item uppon a nother presse in the said wardrop v Cupbord Clothis of olde Conterfait Arras, iij new Cupbord Clothis of Rede Saye, a hoole pece of grene Saye lyred and Sumwhat Worne, ij peces of the Same Cut and lyred, iij Cut peces of new Rede Saye lyred, a pece of new Rede saye wherof part is Cut, a Conterpoint of new Rede saye, iiij peces of olde Rede Saye iij lyred and oon unlyred, iiij olde hinginges of blew Saye lyred, ij bankers of blewe **[p.12]** Saye, xx Single hillinges of verdurs for Cusshens, ij olde hillinges for Cusshens with flourdelices.

Item a Chest in the said wardrop with Stuffe for the Chapell. Furst ij Surplices for men, v Surplices for Children, a Crosse of Coper gilte with a foote and a Shaft of the same, ij Corpras hillinges oon of Clothe of golde and a nother of blewe damaske, ij Auter fruntelettes of olde Stayned worke oon of the Assumpcion of our lady and a nother of the Coronacion of our lady, a lytell Chales with a patent gilte broken, a nother Chales with a patent parcell gilte, a Smale Shippe with a spone therin parcell gilte, a lytell Chapell bell Silver and gilte, ij good Cantercops of blewe velvet barrid with Clothe of golde, a Stayned vestement without an Aulbe, vj Auter frunteletes of Flaxen Clothe with Rede Crosses of bokeram, ij Auter fruntelettes of grene Satyn and Rede Sarsenet, an auter fruntelet of Rede Sarsenet Stayned with a figure of the Trinite, ij Sepulcre Clothis oon of Rede Sarsenet Stayned and a nother of blake bokeram Stayned, an olde Cope of blake Sarsenet Stayned, ij good Cantercopes of bawdekin barred with white velvet and browdred with Sonny[s] of golde, iij Curtens for the Auters ende oon off flaxen Clothe and ij of Sarsenet, ij litell pillows of white Clothe for the Auter, a vaille of flaxen Clothe with a Rede Crosse, vj orfures of bawdekyn and iiij orfures of blew velvet, a good Coope of blewe velvet fentid with Cloth of golde, ij white vestementes for lenten, a good vestement off of bawdekyn, ij Auter Fruntelettes of damask brodured with a Crucifix and Crownys of golde And ij Auter fruntelettes of blak bokeram stayned.

[p.13] Item under the said Wardrop is the Treserhouse.
Item under that a Chambre Callid the nursery with a bedstede therin and nothing els. Item under that a Dungeon and nothing therin.

Item next that betwixt the said Toure and a nother Toure is the great Chambre houngen with vj peeces of blew Saye unlined, A Ceeler, Tester and Curtens of blew bokeram with a Conterpoint of blew Saye, a federbed with a bolster of the same, ij blankettes, ij Sheetes of ij bredes, ij Coverlettes, a Carpet for the window and a Cusshen of verdures, a Chayre, a Spruce Table and a nother Table with iiij formes, a Cupbord Clothe of olde Tapestry Warke. And in an olde Cheste in the said Chamber [*a total of ten diaper table cloths, twenty diaper towels, two towels of new diaper, and nineteen diaper napkins; in ones and twos, except for two lots of four and five towels respectively, and one lot of 17 napkins.*]
Item under that a howse Callid the Dorter that yomen lyeth in with iij bedstedes and iij mattres, iij bolsters of woll [p.14] iij pair of blankettes, iij pair of Sheetes of ij bredes, vj Coverlettes, and iij void bedstedes and nothing els.
Item under that a Storhowse with Chariettes and harnesse for the same, boordes, Leede, Iron, Stoles, fourmes, and moche other broken geere, the keye in the keeping of Robart Fornebe porter of the Holte.
Item Betwixst the said great Chambre and the Chapell a Closet with a Countyngboorde, a Crosbowe with a bending therto, with diverse glasses with watres and diverse Smale Almerys for lettres and billis.

Item next that the Chapell Toure. In the upper Chambre a federbed and a bolster of the same, a pair of Fustians, a pair a Sheetes of iij bredes, ij Coverlettes, a Conterpoint of Rede saye, a Sperver of bawdekyn with Curtens of grene Sarsenet, hongen with ij [peces *deleted*] olde peeces of grene Saye with a Cupborde Clothe of the Same and a Cusshen of grene verdures.

Item uppon a paillet in the same Chambre a mattres and a bolster of woll, ij blankettes, ij Sheetes of ij bredes and ij Coverlettes.

Item under that the Chapell, with a Masbooke, a prosessioner, ij Silver Crewettes, a Sensure of Coper gilte, a Vestement of grene velvet with an Aulbe and an Amyse, ij Auter clothis and a Towell, ij olde Carpettes, iij Cusshens of Crimosyn velvet and ij Cusshens of Conterfait Aras, viij peces of newe Rede Saye browdred with garters and his Reason uppon thaim, Whiche the Chapell is hengen with.

[p.15] Item under that the Stewardes Chambre with an olde fedderbed, ij blankettes and ij Coverlettes which the said Sir William Stanley gave him.

Item under that a nother Chambre with a bedstede and nothing els.

Item under that a Doungeon Callid Pottrels pitte.

Item betwixt the said Toure and the next Toure is the halle, hongen with viij peeces of blew Saye browdred with hartes heedes and his Reason, lyned with Canvas thourow out, an olde Cupbord Clothe and iij Tables with Trestelis and fourmes to the same.

Item under that is the lawe wardrop with iij hinginges of Rede Saye with Swannys on thaim unlyned, with a Conterpoint and Cupbord clothe of the same, iiij litell hinginges of Conterfait Arras olde, with a Conterpoint of the same lyned, vj Carpettes of diverse Sortes somme more summe lesse wherof iij be Right good. In a Cofre in the said Wardrop xvj pair of Sheetes of ij bredes. In a nother Cofre viij pair of Sheetes of ij bredes, and iiij pair and a Sheete of iij bredes, [*blank*] White Coverlettes for servantes, a Conterpoint of White Twilte, xvij good Federbedes and xiij bolsters, x mattres and x bolsters of woll of new Stuffe, ij pakkes of new fedders, v Cut peces of olde Carpettes, a Rounde pavylion, ij pillows of downe, iij Trouncques in oon of thaim a white harnes Complet, a panier Covered with ledder with a pair of brigandynes Coverid with Clothe of golde, a nother panyer with a Cote of plate and a paunchard of blak fustian, ij Jakettes oon of ledder and a nother of Russet [p.16] Clothe, a sertain pecis of white harnes, a bicoket [set *(p.44)*] with silver Studdes [a Sword, ij hingers, dager *(p.44)*] a Clotheseke and iij litell peces of Stained Imagery, iiij olde Sheetes of hollande ij of ij bredes and ij of iij bredes, an olde horsharnes of blake velvet, a great Crosbowe with a windase, ij peces of lyre, ij Bagges of vertgrese, A pair of goldsmyths bellows. And in a gardinyan a horsharnes Coveryd with blak velvet, Furst an hedstall with iij boucles gilte, a patrell with v belles gilte and iiij boucles, A brod Raynes with viij bellis and ij boucles gilte, A Croper with viij bellis and ij boucles gilte, and a pendent to the same with xij bellis and a great belle

Item under that a howse with viij bedstedes and nothing [else *(p.44)*].

Item under that a Stable and a nother house and no[thing *(p.44)*] in thaim.

Item next that at the nedder ende of the halle a Toure Callid the kechin Toure. In the upper Chambre ij mattres, ij bolsters of woll, ij pair of Sheetes of ij bredes and iiij Coverlettes.

Item under that a nother Chambre with a Ceeler and Tester of blake[5] Bokeram And Curtens of the same, with a Conterpoint of blew Saye, hungen with ij olde peces of Rede Saye.

Item under that a nother Chambre with a mattres and a bolster of woll, ij blankettes, ij Sheetes of ij bredes and ij Coverlettes.

Item under that a dungeon and nothing therin.

Item next that at the halle ende is the pantre with ij great **[p.17]** Saltes*[6] with a Cover gilte, a [iiij *(p.45)*] Square Salte without a Cover gilte, a lytell Salte gilte for brekfastes, a Cup* with a Cover gilte Chassid havyng a Crowne a boute the Cover and a nother about the foote, A nother Cup* with a Covere gilt Chassid with the Armes of Woscestre, A pair of Coverid basens* gilte Chassid with Roosys and Sonnys and the Armes of Woscestre in the bothoms, ij Chaffing disshes* Silver with pannys of Iron, ij pair of kervingknyves, a Spone gilt and xv Spones white, x Napkyns* of diaper, ij Towels diaper, a fyne Table Clothe* diaper, ij other Tableclothis diaper, ij Table Clothis of hollande, ix brede[7] Towels, And a great bynne for brede.

Item under that the buttery with ij Standing Cuppis with Covers gilte, A Cup of assaye gilte, vj bollis with a Cover parcell gilte, a White pece parcell gilte and a lytell White pece with a Cover, iiij pottes white oon wantyng a Cover, xx ledder pottes for Ale, iij dripping Tubbis, a great bottel of ledder and a lytell gardinyan empty [vj Standes for ale great and Smale and iiij hoggeshedes [for Ale *(interlined on p.45)*].

Item under that a Wyne Celler and nothin therin.

Item at the Staire heede on the Right hande goyng into the halle is the Ewary with a basyn of Silver parcell gilte of new plate poisaunte [*blank*]

Item a nother mache to the same pois' [*blank*]

Item an olde basen parcell gilte with a Roose in the bothome pois' [*blank*]

Item ij Ewers parcell gilte pois' [*blank*]

Item a White Shaving basen and an Ewer to the same pois' [*blank*]

[p.18] Item vj Tableclothis for the halle, iiij Towells, xxvij Cours Napkins, ij Tourchis, ij Chaffers of brasse and viij Candelstikes of latton.

The utter Courte

Furst a Brewe howse in the said Courte with ix leedes sett in Timbre for worte of oon Sorte, a great Yelling[8] fatte, ij Smale Tubbis and a Clensyng Sinc, and in a nother house a great leede Set in a fournes, a great mashefatt, iij leedes of oon Sorte Set in a frame, a Bras panne. And a bedstede in the said house with a mattres and a bolster of woll.

Item next that the Bakehouse with an oven, ij moulding bordes, a bultyng pipe, ij kneding trowghs, iiij Tubbis for mele, a Sive and a bultyng Clothe.
Item next that a Slaughter house and nothing therin.
Item next that the kilne with a haire to the same.
Item next that a Stable, next the stable an oxe house. And next that iiij Stables.
Item next that a Stoore house with sertayn bordes and a spindle of a Mille.
[p.19] Item next that the Pultre houses and a Chambre for the Pulter, with ij olde Sheetes and ij olde Coverlettes.
Item next that the Garners with malte, wherof of Otten malte by estimacion CLx bushels and of barley malte by Estimacion xL bushels.
Item next that the gatehouse, wherof the upper Chambre is for prisonners, and nothing therin.
Item under that oon the oon syde of the gate is a Chambre for the hunte and the Cater, with a mattres and a bolster of woll, ij blankettes, ij Sheetes and ij Coverlettes.
Item on the other side of the gate is the porters logge, with a mattres and a bolster of woll, ij blanketes, ij Sheetes and ij Coverlettes.
Item next that a barne for Corne, with a baye and a half full of Whete and a quantite of Ottes. Item next that another Barne with haye.
Item next that the Courte house, wherof the lofte is a garner, and a sertayn whete therin.

[p.20] Memorandum that at the veu takin by the said Commissioners at Ridley the xxvijth Daye of January the xth yere of the Raigne of our Souveraigne lorde king Henry the vijth All thise percelles of Stuff and goodes Insuyng war founde in the said place, as it apperith by Indenture betwixt the said Commissioners and the keeper of the said place.
Furst ij basens Silver and gilte, iij basens Silver parcell gilte, ij Ewers parcell gilte, iij pottes Silver for wine, ij Cuppes with ij Covers oon of thaim gilte, iij Silver Candelstikes, ij Auter Candelstikes of Silver, a Chales with a patent gilte, a pax with ij Crewettes Silver and gilte, iij plain Cuppis ij of thaim gilte, xxiiij Spones Silver, A masbook with all Stuffe for the Auter for oon prest, the Chapell hongen with grene Saye browdred with garters and parcell therof bawdekyn, iij peces of Conterfait Ares for hinginges for the parlour, hinginges for the hall and Chambres xxvij. Item iij other peeces of Conterfait Ares or Aras the keeper Cannot tell unto they be Sene. Item sertain peeces of Saye wherof the nombre is not as yet known for it is not in the place. Item viij fedderbedes with bolsters therto, xviij mattres with bolsters therto, xviij pair of blankettes of white Clothe,

iij pair of fustians, xviij pair of Sheetes, iij pair of the same fyne Sheetes, xij Cusshens of Conterfait Ares. Item iiij Cushens of Silk and oon of Clothe of golde, xiiij pillows, a garnishe of pewter vessell, iij Spittes of Irn, ij litell Spittes, ij gawbertes of Iron [viij pottes, viij pannys, ij fleshokkes, ij pothillinges, ij Table clothis. Item a Table clothe diaper werke, ij litell diaper Towels, xxiiij Coverlettes, ij Coverynges for beddes of Silke, ij Coveringes for bedds of Conterfait Aras, iij Spervers of Silke, iij Spervers of white clothe, A draw bedde without Curtens and a glasse in a table uppon the auter in the Chapell. The Substaunce of thise goodes be comyn into (this *deleted*) the Castell of the Holte *(pp.48-49)*.]

[p.21 absent]
[p.22] Stuffe Trussid as Folloith
Furst a federbed out of the laughe wardrop of with a bolster of the marke   R
Item a Federbed and a bolster of the marke of   O
Item a Federbed and a bolster of the marke of   N
Item a Federbed and a bolster of the mark of   P
Item a Federbed and a bolster of the marke   O [?]
Item a Federbed and bolster of the marke   Q
Item a Federbed and a pillow from Ridley of the marke   S
Item a Federbed and a pillow which pillow come from Ridley of the marke   F
Item a Federbed and ij pillows which pillows came from Ridley of the marke   M
Item a Federbed and a pillow which pillowe came from Ridley of the marke   L
Item a Federbed and a pillow whiche pillowe came from Ridley of the marke   H
Item a Federbed and a pillowe which pillowe came from Ridley of the marke   K
Item a Federbed and a bolster which came from Ridley of the marke   P
Item a Federbed and a bolster out of the great Chambre of the Holte
of the marke   I
Item a Federbed and a bolster which came from Ridley of the marke   A
Item a Federbed and a bolster out of the Chapel Chambre of the marke   G
Item a Federbed and a bolster of the marke   T
Item a Federbed out of the glasiers Toure and a pillow from Ridley D
         of the marke
Item a Federbed and a bolster out of the laugh Wardrop of the marke   B
[p.23] Item of the Stuffe of the Treserhouse, ij Covered basons gilte, iij basons white, a litel Coffre with Juelx and a Case with plate, and out of the Ewary ij basens and an ewer, out of the buttery iiij bollis with a cover white, and from Ridley ij Covered basens, a Federbed and iij bolsters, ij pillows wherof oon is of Ridley of the marke of v   [V *at right hand side of para.*]
Item trussid in a Clothsek a good bedde of bawdekyn with Swannys of golde with a Counterpoint of the same, a Sperver of panys of blew velvet and white damaske,

a Sperver of bawdekyn and ij Spervers of Cloth of golde, a good parlament Robe of Scarlet furrid with myneveir and a hoode to the same, and ij Mantels of Saint George of blew velvet lyned with white sersenet.

Furst x peeces of verdures bordured with olde tentes and ij peeces of palle verdures of the marke   j

Item iij peces of verdures with Connys, ij peces of pale verdures, a litell pece of verdur, ij peces of conterfait Arras of the Story of Olifernus of the nombre   ij

Item a pece of Conterfait Arras of the Story of David and oon peece of Olifernus of the nombre   iij

Item a pece of Conterfait Arras of the Story of Davyd and iiij peeces of verdures with Fowlys and wilde bestes of the nombre   iiij

Item ij peces of verdures with Fowlys and wilde bestes, iij peeces of Conterfait Arres of the Sege of Jerusalem and a Conterpoint of Smale verdures of the nombre   v

[p.24] Item a Ceeler and tester of Conterfait Arras out of the highe Wardrop and v peeces of Rede verdurs with an Egle and a childe in the nest that came from Ridley of the nombre   vj

Item iiij peeces of Rede verdures, iiij peeces of grene verdures and a pece of pale verdures whiche came from Ridley of the nombre   vij

Item ij peeces of pale verdures and vij peeces of conterfait arres that came from Ridley of the nombre   viij

Item v carpettes wherof ij came from Rideley, ij Cusshens of Crimosyn velvet barred with Clothe of gold, a Cusshen of Clothe of golde whiche came from Rideley and iij Cusshens of blewe bawdekyn, and out of the Wardrop a Cusshen of Russet Clothe of golde, a Cusshen of blewe bawdekyn and ij tapettes oon of Rede and a nother of blak Fured with mynevier, of the nombre   ix

Item xj peeces of Olde Rede Saye and vj of olde worne grene Saye, xij peeces of olde blewe saie great and Smale, a pece of Reede Saye and an olde Conterpoint of white Saye of the nombre   x

Item xxj pair of Sheetes of iij bredes, xij pair of Sheetes and a sheete of ij bredes and iij olde Rede hinginges of Rede with Swannys in thaim which came from Ridley, of the nombre   xj

Item vij peces of olde grene Saye, iiij peeces of olde blewe Saye, iij peeces of Rede Saye, ij pair of olde Fustians, ij olde pales of grene velvet browdered with Flourdelices, a Celer and iij peeces of olde Conterfait Arres of the nombre   xij

[p.25] Item vij peeces of Olde conterfait Arras, iij olde Cusshens of Bawdekyn out of the wardrop, a Curten of tawney sarsenet, iij Curtens of blewe Taffetas, a Curten of Rede Taffetas, a nother of grene and a nother of blake, ij olde worne Carpettes, iij olde cupbord clothis of conterfait Arras, v bankers of verdures, a Sparver of blew bokeram which came from Ridley, v hillinges of Cusshens and v Sheetes of the nombre   xiij

Item a good peece of conterfait Arras of the Seege of Jerusalem, a Cope of blewe velvet broderid, ij Auterclothis of bawdekin, ij Cantercopis of velvet, a Corperas of Clothe of golde, a vestement of blew Damaske with an Aulbe to the same, ij quarters of purpel velvet uppon velvet, a gowne of the same velvet, iiij gownes of velvet of the same colour, a Mantel for a Woman of the same velvet, a Conterpoint of Saloman, a Jaket of golde smyths work, which Stuffe come out of the high Wardrop, a Sperver of bawdekyn with Courtens of grene Sarsene, iij pillowes of downe and a Fustian which came out of the Chapel Chambre, of the nombre   xiiij

[p.26]   Juelx plate and money founde founde [sic] in the Tresorhouse.

Furst an olde Chales with a patent gilte with Imagery, a paxe with iij Images gilte, a Cup of golde Chassid with vij perles, iiij Standing Cuppis gilte, vj Smale playn bollis with a Cover gilte, ij pottes writhen gilte, ij Flagons with Chaines gilte, ij faire Saltes with a cover gilte, a faire Flagon gilte wanting half the handel, a litel leyer gilte, a Case with vj bollis and a Cover parcel gilte, a bason parcel gilte, ij Saltes with a Cover parcel gilte, a litel Standing cup with a Cover parcel gilte, a Chassid peece with a Cover parcel gilt, a Covering of a pece gilte wantyng a knop, a litel paxe gilte, ij basons white, iiij Ewers parcel gilte, a great white bolle for a posset, iiij peeces white, iij Candelstikes white, vj bollis with a Cover white, a potte parcel gilte, ij Crewettes parcel gilte, a case with a deepe bason white, vj goblettes with a Cover white, an ewer white, a litel Salte parcel gilte with a Cover, a Spone and a fork for grene ginger and ij masers.

Item in an olde Spruce cofre ix brode olde Corsis without harnes, a good corse harnessid with Silver and gilte, ij olde Corsis harnessid with Silver and gilte, with other bagage of no value.

Item a nother Spruce Cofre with a Salte of byral and gold garnisshed with Stone and perle, a Salte of golde and Jasper wel garnisshid with Stone and perle, a nother Salte of golde Garnisshid with Smale perles, a great brode chayne of golde, a Crucifix with iij Images Silver and gilte, iij Spones gilte, a ginger boxe parcel gilte, a powdre boxe with the kinges Armes parcel gilte, Reliques Closid in a litel Tablet of Silver, a litel paxe with Saint George gilte, in the said Coffre a litel Coffre and therin a litel corse garnisshid with Silver and gilte, iiij Ringes of gold with Turkes, a Ring of gold with a Crapawde, a litel Ring of gold with a Leopardes face, a Ring of golde with a Jac..cce, a Ring with a course diamond, a Ring with a Topase, ij playn hoopis of gold, a harte of gold with a course Amatise, a litel praty Cofre of Silver fful of Course Stones, a litel loker with ij braunchis of golde and a perle in oon of thaim, a table Silver and gilt with iij leves, a Claspe for a gurdel, the garnisshing of Colier gold white Roosys and the Sonne broken. Item a longe Coffre with xxxij peeces of fyne Lynnen of Sheetes and othir thing. Item ther lieth wonden togidder in a Sheete a dowblet of Clothe of golde wantyng a Sleve and diverse othir peeces of Silk and velvet for vestementes and other bagage.

[p.27]   Insueth the Content of the bagges

> *[There were* 139 *bags, containing a total of*   £9161.7s.3d.
> *This included one bag with £254.19s.2d. in gold, two bags with £42 and £23 in groats (4d pieces) and two bags containing £64 and £46 in pence.]*

NOTES

1   Squier *deleted.*
2   ij *(p.33)*
3   Item a good Sperver of bawdekyn with Curtens of grene Sarsenet is inserted in another hand at the bottom of the page and then deleted.
4   16 pairs plus one, i.e. 33 sheets.
5   Blew (p.45).
6   * Noted at these points "Delivered to H. Wiat," "delivered to H," "Item delivered" etc.
7   Possibly *brode.*
8   yeillyng *(p.46).*

GLOSSARY OF TERMS USED IN THE INVENTORY

Almerys	aumbry, pl. aumbries: a repository, storehouse, cupboard (in a wall or article of furniture), a safe, locker, press.
amatise	amethyst
amyse	amice: rectangular piece of white linen worn around the neck and shoulders by the priest during Mass, put on over the alb (q.v. under Aulbe)
aulbe	alb: full-length white linen garment worn beneath the other vestments by the priest during Mass
auter frontlettes	altar frontal: coloured cloth hanging in front of altar.
Bawdekyn	baudekin: a rich silk brocade
bicoket	bycocket: a cap of estate; a hat cocked (folded) up on two sides.
boll, bolle, bollis	bowl(s)
bordes	boards
bordured	bordered
boucles	buckles
brede, bredes	breadth(s); bread

brigandynes	brigandine: body armour composed of iron rings or small thin iron plates, sewn upon canvas, linen or leather, and covered with similar material.
brode	broad
browdered	embroidered
bultyng	bolting (i.e. sieving). Bolting cloth: cloth for sieving flour.
Cantercopes	*poss.* cope: church vestment of silk, usually semicircular in shape.
caparike	caperik, caprike: a kind of wine
cape de hustys	[unknown]
cater	[unknown]
celer, seler	canopy of bed
chaffer	*poss.* chafing-dish
chales	chalice
chamelet	chamelot, chamlet, camlot: fine fabric, often mixed silk and wool
charnettes	charne: obsolete form of churn
chassid	chased: embossed, engraved
chequre	exchequer
clotheseke	cloth sack? clothes sack?
cofre	coffer
coks	cooks, cook's
connys, conys	coneys, rabbits
coope	cope
corperas	corporal: small square of linen cloth spread on the altar during Mass.
corse, corsis, corsys	*poss.* body armour
conterfait aras	counterfeit Arras: imitation of tapestry woven in Arras in Flanders.
counterpoint	counterpane
cours	coarse
crapawd	toadstone
crewettes	cruets: pair of small altar vessels holding wine and water before they are mixed for consecration during Mass
croper	crupper: item of horse harness passing under the horse's tail
cupbord	a sideboard, used to display silver dishes etc
Depnes	deepness
dorter	dormitory
dousyn	dozen
Fentid	*poss.* edged, *poss.* slit
flourdelise	fleur de lys
formes, fourmes	forms, benches
fournes	furnace
frees	frieze: coarse cloth
fustian	thick, twilled linen cloth
Gardinyan	[unknown but poss. trunk or chest]
garner	granary
garnishe	set of pewter vessels and dishes for table use
garters	strap and buckle design, the badge of the Order of the Garter
gawbertes	irons for supporting the spit in front of the fire; iron racks for chimneys

Haire	[unknown]
hillinges	hilling: a covering, protection
hinginges	hangings
hogges hedes	hogshead: a liquid measure, now a beer measure of 54 gallons
hollande	holland: a linen fabric
Jarmit	poss. garnet
journet	[unknown, poss. jacket]
Kendall	kendal: coarse woollen or linen fabric usually coloured green
Latton	latten: alloy of copper, zinc, lead and tin, similar to fine brass
laugh, laughe, lawe	low
lawse	[unknown]
leedes	[unknown]
logge	lodge
lyre, lyred	cloth from a town in Brabant
Maser	drinking-cup made of maple or sycamore wood
mashefatt	a vat used in the malting process
mynever	miniver: fur from the white belly skins of the Baltic squirrel
Nedder	nether, lower
Olyfarnos	Holofernes, slain by Judith (Old Testament)
orfures	orphreys: decorative garment-edgings, originally of goldwork, later of rich fabric or embroidery
Paillet	pallet, palliasse: straw mattress or small bed stuffed with straw
panys	panes: wide strips
parcell gilt	parcel gilt: partly gilded, especially of silverware such as bowls and cups having the inner surface gilded
parlament robe	robe of state, worn usually by members of Parliament. (N.B.Sir William Stanley was not an MP but wore such a robe at the investiture of Arthur as Prince of Wales)
patent	patten: shallow dish used during Mass, on which the consecrated Host rests. Usually gold or gilded.
patrell	[unknown]
paunchard	pauncher: part of armour of 14th and 15th centuries, covering lower part of body
paxe	pax: small tablet with representation of crucifixion, kissed at Mass by priest and others
poisant(e)	weighing
pipe	liquid measure; a half tun or 2 hogsheads or 4 barrels of wine. Now a beer measure of 108 gallons. (NB a barrel is now a beer measure of 36 gallons)
posnet	small saucepan with three legs, made to stand at the edge of a fire
poudring	powdering: salting, to preserve meat.
prosessioner	processioner: a book containing the texts and music used during processions in church or chapel
pulter	poultry-keeper
Reason	motto

Sangwyn	sanguine: blood-red colour
sarsenet	fine soft silk cloth. By a statute of Edward IV the wives and unmarried daughters of persons having possessions of the yearly value of £20 or upwards were permitted "to use and were in their colers, ventes and slefes of their gownes and hukes sateyn chamelet sarcenet or tarteron."
saye	fine, serge-like cloth
scante	scant. A scant yard: barely a yard, no surplus.
sensure	censer, thurible (container in which incense is burnt)
sepulchre clothes	coverings for Easter Sepulchre in church or chapel, where consecrated Host was kept from Good Friday to Easter Sunday.
serpentyne	serpentine: kind of cannon, used largely as ship's gun.
shippe	ship; here, incense-boat, or container from which incense is measured into the censer (q.v. under sensure) or thurible for burning.
soussing	pickling
sperver	sparver: canopy or tester of a bed. Whole frame of bed, to which the curtains, valances etc were attached, not the canopy or tester only
stayned	painted, usually with image of saint etc or Scripture scene. A less costly alternative to tapestry or embroidery.
stoles	stole: a packing chest for robes and clothes. Or stools.
Tester	canopy of a bed
travers	screen with curtains, used in chapels, halls and other large rooms
trestelis	trestles: supporting structures for tables or platforms
trounques	trunks
trowgh	trough
truss	to pack close
turkes	turquoise(s)
twilte	twill: a type of weave for cloth
Unsuyng	ensuing
Vaille	veil, i.e. for use in chapel during Lent, to screen off the altar
verdures	verdures: a particular kind of cloth, perhaps green baize. Apparently woven with flowers etc.
vergeous	verjuice or vinegar
vertgrese	[unknown]
vestement	vestment: garment or set of garments worn by priest and others when saying or serving Mass.
veu	view
Worte	wort
writhen	twisted, or closed
wonden	wound. Wonden togidder: wound together.
Yeilling, yelling	obsolete form of gyling: brewing

❀

Appendix 2

Lathom House

THERE has been some doubt as to the actual location of the manor house of Lathom in the 15th century. One theory has it that the house and its adjacent settlement were on the western edge of the manorial lands, near the boundary with Burscough where the moated remains of a house have been found.[1] This, however, is believed to be the site of Alton or Halton Castle and now designated a hunting lodge in the New Park.[2] But in 1960 the remains that were excavated related to a sixteenth century building.[3] Another theory places the location of the manor house at the site of the later Lathom House which was enlarged and fortified by the first Earl of Derby and visited by Henry VII in 1495.[4] This, Derby House, has now disappeared and at one time was believed to be in Spa Ruff woods.[5] However, the controversy has now been resolved as excavations have taken place adjacent to the remaining wing of Lathom House, built in 1713, and remains have been found which seem to confirm that this is the site of the first Earl of Derby's Lathom House.[6]

NOTES

1 Pilkington, p.14.
2 McCrone, Peter. Talk given to Ormskirk and District Family History Society, November 1999.
3 Steane and Kelsall, pp.73-78. This site is now under Ormskirk Golf Course.
4 Smith and others, p.16.
5 Critchley, pp.43-44.
6 McCrone. See n.2 above. Mark Fletcher, talk to Ormskirk Arch. Soc., May 2003.

Lathom and New Park.
Details adapted from
Saxton's 1577 map of
Lancashire

Bibliography

Manuscript Sources

PRO [Public Record Office] E154/2/5 46406: Inventory of Holt and Ridley.

Printed Sources

ARCHBOLD, W.A.J. "Sir William Stanley and Perkin Warbeck" *in English Historical Review*, vol.14 (1899) pp.529-34.

ARTHURSON, IAN. (1) *The Perkin Warbeck conspiracy, 1491-1499.* 1994.

ARTHURSON, IAN.(2) "A Question of Loyalty" in *Ricardian,* vol.7, no.97 (1987) pp.402-13.

BAGLEY, J.J. *The Earls of Derby 1458-1985.* 1985.

BAYNE, C.G. *and* DUNHAM, W.H. *Select cases in the Council of Henry VII (Court of Star Chamber).* 1956. (Selden Society, vol.75)

BENNETT, M. (1) *The Battle of Bosworth.* 1993.

BENNETT, M. (2) "Henry VII and the Northern Rising of 1489" in *Eng.Hist.Rev.,* vol.105 (Jan.1990) pp.34-59.

BLUNDEN-ELLIS, J. "Sir Edmund Shaa, Kt., P.C." in *Ricardian,* vol.3, no.45 (1974) pp.11-16.

BOARDMAN, A.W. *The Battle of Towton.* 1994.

CALENDAR of Inquisitions Post Mortem, Henry VII vols.1 and 2, Years 1-20.

[CPR] *Calendar of Patent Rolls: Henry VI, vol.6, 1452-1461;Edward IV, 1461-1467; Edward IV and Henry VI, 1467-1477; Edward IV, Edward V and Richard III, 1476-1485; and Henry VII vol.2, 1494-1509.*

CAMPBELL, W. (Ed.) *Materials for a history of the reign of Henry VII from original documents in the Public Record Office.* 2 vols. 1877, rp.1965.

CHEETHAM, A. *The Life and times of Richard III.* 1972.

CHRIMES, S.B. (1) *Fifteenth century England 1399-1509.* 1995.

CHRIMES, S.B. (2) *Henry VII.* 1966.

CHRIMES, S.B. (3) *Lancastrians, Yorkists and Henry VII.* 1966.

CLAYTON, D.J. *Administration of the county palatine of Chester 1442-1485.* Manchester, 1990. (Chetham Society)

COKAYNE, G.E. *The Complete peerage.* 1916.

COLE, H. *The Wars of the Roses.* 1973.

The COMPLETE peerage. See COKAYNE, G.E.

COWARD, B. *The Stanleys, Lords Stanley and Earls of Derby, 1385-1672.* Manchester, 1983. (Chetham Society)

CRITCHLEY, L. *A Study of the township of Lathom in West Lancashire.* (Diploma in Landscape Interpretation, Liverpool University, 1991-92)

CROSTON, J. *County families of Lancashire and Cheshire.* 1887.

CUNNINGHAM, S. "Henry VII and Rebellion in North-eastern England, 1485-1492: Bonds of Allegiance and the Establishment of Tudor Authority" *in Northern History,* vol.31 (1996) pp.42-74.

[DNB] Dictionary of National Biography, *sub nomm.* Sir William Stanley; Francis Lovel; John Tiptoft Earl of Worcester.

DOCKRAY, KEITH, *and* KNOWLES, RICHARD. "The Battle of Wakefield and the Wars of the Roses" in *Ricardian,* vol.9, no.117 (June 1992)

DORLING, E.E. "The Heraldry of the Font at Holt" in *Transactions of the Historic Society of Lancashire and Cheshire,* vol.60 (1908) (N.S.24) pp.97-104.

DRAPER, P. *The House of Stanley including the sieges of Lathom House ....* Ormskirk, 1864.

DREWETT, R. *and* M. REDHEAD, M. *The Trial of Richard III.* 1984.

DRIVER, J.T. *Cheshire in the later Middle Ages, 1399-1540.* 1971.

ELTON, G.R. *England under the Tudors.* 2nd ed. 1974.

EVANS, H.T. *Wales and the Wars of the Roses.* 1995.

FOSS, P.J. *The Field of Redemore: the Battle of Bosworth 1485.* Leeds, 1990.

FOSTER, C. [Guidebook to] *Arley Hall, Cheshire.* Arley, 1982.

GIDMAN, J. "Sir William Stanley of Holt: Who was the Mother of his Children?" in *Ricardian*, vol.10, no.124 (March 1994) pp.21-22. See also PERKINS, J.M., below.

GILL, L. *Richard III and Buckingham's rebellion.* 1999.

GILLESPIE, J.L. "Richard II's Cheshire Archers" in *Trans. Historic Soc. of Lancs. and Cheshire,* vol.125 (1974) pp.1-39.

GREEN, V.H.H. *The Later Plantagenets.* 1966.

GRIFFITHS, R.A. (1) "Patronage, Politics and the Principality of Wales, 1413-1461" in R.A.Griffiths (ed.), *King and country: England and Wales in the fifteenth century.* 1991.

GRIFFITHS, R.A. (2) "Richard of York and the Royal Household in Wales 1449-1450" in R.A. Griffiths (ed.), *King and country.* 1991.

HABBERJAM, MOIRA. "Sir Robert Clifford" in *Blanc Sanglier*, vol.28, no.3 (Aug. 1994) pp.3-5.

HAMMOND, P.W. (1) "Lord Hastings" in *Ricardian*, no.39 (Dec.1972) pp.10-12.

HAMMOND, P.W. (2) "Richard III at York" in *Ricardian*, no.41 (June 1973), pp.3-4.

HAMMOND, P.W. (3) *and others.* "The Reburial of Richard Duke of York, 21-30 July 1976" in *Ricardian*, vol.10, no.127 (1994), pp.122-65.

HAMPTON, W.E. *Memorials of the Wars of the Roses: a biographical guide.* 1979.

HANHAM, A. "Hastings redivivus" in *Eng.Hist.Rev.,* vol.90 (1975) pp.821-27.

HARVEY, N.L. *Elizabeth of York, Tudor queen.* 1973.

HICKS, M.A. "Edward IV, the Duke of Somerset and Lancastrian Loyalism in the North" in *Northern Hist.*, vol.20 (1984) pp.23-37.

HOLINSHED's Chronicle, as used in Shakespeare's plays. Ed. A. and J. Nicoll. 1927, rp. 1975.

HORROX, R. *and* HAMMOND, P.W. *British Library Harleian MS 433.* 4 vols. 1979.

IRVINE, W.F. "The Early Stanleys" in *Trans. Historic Soc. of Lancs. and Cheshire,* vol.105 (1953) pp.45-68.

JAMES, A.J. "An Amended Itinerary to Bosworth Field" in *Ricardian*, vol.9, no.113 (June 1991) pp.54-69.

JONES, M.K. (1) "Sir William Stanley of Holt: Politics and Family Allegiance in the Fifteenth Century" in *Welsh History Review*, vol.14 (1988) pp.1-22.

JONES, M.K. (2) "Sir William Stanley and 'Olde Dyk'" in *Ricardian*, vol.8, no.105 (1989) p.236.

JONES, M.K. *and* UNDERWOOD, M. *The King's mother: Lady Margaret Beaufort, Countess of Richmond and Derby.* 1992.

KENDALL, P.M. (1) *Richard III.* Pb.1972.

KENDALL, P.M. (2) *Warwick the Kingmaker and the Wars of the Roses.* Pb1972

KINROSS, J. *Walking and exploring the battlefields of Britain.* 1988.

LANDER, J.R.(1) "Attainder and Forfeiture 1453 to 1509" in LANDER, J.R. (Ed.) *Crown and nobility 1450-1509.* 1976.

LANDER, J.R. (2) *The Wars of the Roses.* 1990

McKELVEY, E. *Thomas Stanley, first Earl of Derby, 1435-1504.* (Ph.D thesis, Pennsylvania State University, 1966)

McNIVEN, P. "The Men of Cheshire and the Rebellion of 1403" in *Trans. Historic Soc. of Lancs. and Cheshire,* vol.129 (1980) pp.1-29.

MARKHAM, *Sir* CLEMENTS. *Richard III: his life and character.* 1906, rp.1968.

MEDHURST, NANCY. "The Lands of Sir William Stanley" in *Blanc Sanglier,* vol.24, no.1 (Dec.1989) pp.20-21.

MOUNT, TONI. "The Trial of Sir William Stanley, February 1495" in *Blanc Sanglier*, vol.29, no.1 (Dec.1994), pp.10-11.

MYERS, A.R. (1) *The Household of Edward IV: the Black Book and the Ordinance of 1478.* 1959.

MYERS, A.R.(2) "An Official Progress through Lancashire and Cheshire in 1476" in *Trans. Historic Soc. of Lancs. and Cheshire*, vol.115 (1963), pp.1-29.

NICHOLAS, N.H. *The Privy Purse expenses of Elizabeth of York; the Wardrobe accounts of Edward IV.* 1830. Facsim. reprint 1972.

NICHOLS, J. (Ed.) *The Grants of Edward V.* 1854. (Camden Society)

ORMEROD, G. *History of the County Palatine and City of Chester.* 3 vols. 1882.

PACKHAM, C. "Sir Richard Bray and the Crown at Bosworth." Letter in *Ricardian Bulletin,* March 1996, p.31.

PALMER, A.N. *On the town of Holt.* 1907. (*Archaeologia Cambrensis*, 6th Series, vol.7)

PERKINS, J.M. "The Origins and Rise of the Stanley Family" in *Blanc Sanglier,* vol.13, no.1 (Dec.1978) pp.3-6. See also GIDMAN, J., above.

PEVSNER, N. and HUBBARD, *The Buildings of England: Cheshire.* 1971.

PILKINGTON, C. *To play the man.* Preston, 1991.

POLLARD, A.J. *Richard III and the Princes in the Tower.* 1991.

ROGERS, C. *Henry VII.* 1991.

SEACOME. *History of the House of Stanley.* Manchester, 1821.

SHAW, W.A. *The Knights of England. Vol. 1: Knights of the Garter.* 1906.

SKEEL, C.A.J. *The Council in the Marches of Wales.* 1904. (Girton College Studies, no.2)

SMITH, G. "Lambert Simnel and the king from Dublin" in *Ricardian,* vol.10 no.135 (Dec.1996) pp.498-536.

SMITH, J.B. "Crown and Community in the Principality of North Wales in the Reign of Henry VII" in *Welsh Hist. Rev.,* vol.3 part 2 (1966) pp.145-71.

SMITH, P. *and others. A short history of Lathom.* 1981.

STARKEY, D. "Intimacy and Innovation: the Rise of the Privy Chamber 1485-1547" in

STARKEY, D. (Ed.), *The English court from the Wars of the Roses to the Civil War.* 1987.

STEANE, J.M. and KELSALL, A.F. "The Park, Moat and House at New Park, Lathom, near Ormskirk" in *Trans. Historic Soc. of Lancs. and Cheshire,* vol.114 (1962) pp.73-78.

SUTTON, A.F. and HAMMOND, P.W. *The Coronation of Richard III.* 1983.

SUTTON, A.F. and VISSER-FUCHS, L. "The Royal Burials of the House of York at Windsor - Edward IV" in *Ricardian*, vol.11, no.143 (1998) pp.366-407.

TAYLOR, A.J. *King's works in Wales* 1277-1330. 1974.

THORNTON, T. "The Integration of Cheshire into the Tudor Nation State in the Early Sixteenth Century" in *Northern Hist.,* vol.29 (1993) pp.40-63.

VIRGOE, R. "The benevolence of 1481" in *Eng.Hist.Rev.*, vol.104, no.410 (1989) pp.25-45.

WHEELER, G. *The Battle of Tewkesbury: a roll of arms.* 1971.

WHITE, W.J. "The Death and Burial of Henry VI" in *Ricardian*, vol.6, no.78 (1982) pp.70-80.

WILLIAMS, J. *The Stanley family of Lathom and Knowsley c.1450-1504.* (M.A. thesis, Manchester Univ., 1979.)

WILLIAMS, N. *The Life and times of Henry VII.* 1973.

WILSON, K.P. (Ed.) *Chester Customs accounts 1301-1566.* 1969. (Record Society of Lancs. and Cheshire, vol.111)

Index

Richard, Duke of York, s. of Edward IV
18-20, 23, 29-32, 57-59
Richmond, Earl of *see* Tudor
Earldom of 35
Ridley 4, 21, 40-41, 44-45, 47, 50-51, 58,
62, 70-72
Rivers, Earl *see* Woodville, Anthony
Robin of Redesdale 9
Roby 1
Rotherham, Thomas, Archbishop of York
18
Rouen 2
Rugeley 25
Ruyabon [Ruabon] 45

St. Albans 11
First Battle of (1455) 2-3
Second Battle of (1461) 5
St Winefride's Well 47
Salisbury 20
Earl of *see* Neville, Richard
Salop (Shropshire) 45-46, 58
Sandwich 4
Savage, Sir Humphrey 57-58
Sir John, marr. Catharine Stanley
3, 40, 57
Sir John, s. of above 25
Scotland 21, 39
Scottish Borders 10
Sessewik 45
Severn, River 11-12
Shaa, Edmund 19
Dr. Ralph 19
Sheen 33
Sheepy Magna 25
Sheriff Hutton 21
Shrewsbury 25, 46
Simnel, Lambert 32-33, 55
Skipton in Craven 7, 13, 45, 57, 59
Snowdon 43
Sodor and Man, Bishopric of 1
Sonford 45
South Wales *see* Wales
Stafford 25
Stafford, Edward, Duke of Buckingham 30,
58
Henry, Duke of Buckingham 17-20, 23,
30, 44-45
Sir Henry 12

Stafford, Humphrey 31
Thomas 31
Stanley, Staffs. 1
Tower 1
Stanley, Catharine, marr. Sir John Savage
3, 40, 57
Catherine, marr. Thomas Cocat 51, 52
Sir Edward 50, 62
Sir Edward, s. of Sir Thomas 16
Eleanor, Lady Strange 33
Elizabeth, marr. Sir Richard Molyneux 2
Elizabeth, marr. Sir Peter Warburton 52
George, Lord Strange 22, 24-26, 45, 56
James, Archdeacon of Carlisle 2
Joan (Beaumont), marr.William Stanley
of Holt 8, 41, 49, 51, 54, 55
Joan (1493-1570) 51
Joan, marr. John Warburton 41, 52
Joan, mother of William ap William ap
Griffith 43
John, Constable of Caernarfon Castle 43
John, marr. Elizabeth Weever 2
Sir John, b.1340 1, 4, 37, 49, 53
Sir John, b.1386 1
Margaret 2
Thomas, s. of Sir William 53, 58
Sir Thomas, 1st Lord Stanley 2, 37-38,
43-44
Sir Thomas, 2nd Lord Stanley 2-4, 7-8,
10, 12-14, 16-27, 29-30, 33-34, 38,
40-41, 45-46, 53, 56, 60
William de 1
William (IV) 1
William (V) 1
Sir William of Holt *passim*
Sir William of Hooton 43
William, s. of Sir William of Holt 51, 59
Stoke, Battle of (1487) 32, 34-35, 55
Stone 25
Stony Stratford 17
Storeton, Wirral 1
Stotwick Park 41
Strange *see* Stanley, Eleanor *and* George
Suffolk 20
Duke of *see* Pole, de la
Sutton Cheney 25-26
Sutton Hall 52
Swynford, Katherine, Duchess of Lancaster
12